HOW TO TRANSFORM
YOUR LOVE LIFE

KIMBERLEY HEART

Published by Unlimited Consulting Inc. All Right Reserved
P.O. 28712, Las Vegas, NV 89126

Cover Design: Tracy Van Dolder, Virtually Possible Designs
Edited by: Jeff Lyons, www.storygeeks.com
Line Editor: Elinor Perry-Smith, (Twitter) @BrideOfChrist
Book design: Michelle Glush

First Printing, 2014
ISBN 978-0-9916655-1-8

Contents

This book is for you—yes you…

…the one who is courageous enough to risk love and more,

who wants to have the insight, skills and beliefs to keep it.

You are the reason I share my journey.

Kimberley Heart

Gratitude

I have been blessed with not one, but two mentors who have superseded all expectations of loyalty, steadfastness, patience, and most of all, love. There will never be words big enough to express my gratitude to you both.

Lazaris, for thirty-four years now you have held my hand and told me of my love and brilliance. You have had immense patience with my failings and have everlasting belief in me. I love you. I am eternally grateful that you called me and I found you. I love you more than I can express.

Baratta, you have helped me move into new paradigms of myself. You have steadfastly shared with me, in ways I could best receive, the lessons that would help me be the woman I wanted to be. I love you, and that one moment will last forever.

To you both I owe the quality of my life and am eternally grateful.

Kimberley's Note

CHANGE: Utilizing the Power of Our Subconscious Mind

One of the fastest ways to grow and change is to get our subconscious mind to help. We can achieve this by learning the language our subconscious mind understands. Our subconscious mind language is metaphor, color, sound, intensity of emotions, immense focus, and our directives.

We will discuss the subconscious mind more in Chapter 10. Currently, I believe the best way to achieve the goal of accessing the power of our subconscious mind is to use visualization or meditation to communicate with it.

Meditation is simply one way to get our minds to slow down in order to absorb information more clearly, thereby allowing us to discover more about ourselves. However, slowing down our minds takes practice.

Two Types of Meditation

There are two basic kinds of meditation: *guided meditation* and *clear mind meditation*. *Guided meditation* is a team effort between you and the person leading the meditation, whether in person or listening to a recording. Guided meditation can take us on a journey filled with color, sound, smell, touch, taste and feelings. If the meditation is well done, it will utilize as many senses as possible and as many feelings as are appropriate. This is my favorite kind of meditation.

I have chosen to use guided meditation in this book because I have found it to be one of the fastest, most powerful avenues to change. The two meditations shared in the *Meditations* section on page 217 are examples of this.

For the sake of clarity, I will briefly mention the second type of meditation. *Clear mind meditation* is used to clear the mind of all thought. There are many ways to achieve this but it is not our focus here.

Secret

The secret to the success of any meditation is the depth and intensity of our emotions; the combination of our thoughts and feelings. Feelings are the conduit between us and our subconscious mind. Our emotions tell our subconscious mind that we want to communicate. In fact, our feelings are one of the only ways our subconscious mind can differentiate between benign, daily existence and our intent to communicate with it.

However, meditation in itself is not a panacea. Meditation alone can only accomplish so much. That is why it is important to use meditation in conjunction with other tools. This is the purpose of the Homegrowths that you will discover in select chapters. Homegrowths is a term with which you may not be familiar. They are exercises that give you the opportunity to grow and—if you are willing—to change.

A note to you, the reader!

It is essential to complete Part One of this book, *before* moving on to Part Two and the guided meditations, which are presented in detail in the *Meditations* section. It is the synergy of these tools, the Homegrowths and the meditations, that creates lasting change. Part Two provides a detailed example of Homegrowths, which you can use as a model in your own development. If you jump ahead without understanding the context for change, you will undermine the quantum growth of which you are capable, and which you deserve.

PART ONE:
OUR LOVE STORY

CHAPTER ONE:

In the Beginning

WE BOTH set out to love.

To love takes immense courage. Sometimes you have to leave behind all you know, and all that you believe in order to find yourself, and then to find love. I wasn't always courageous, nor was he. Yet, we both jumped in heart first. As with so many modern love stories, ours began through an introduction online:

Jeff: Kimberley ru interested in meeting a man?
Kimberley: Yes, why?
Jeff: Because I might have a ringer 4u.

Everything I'm about to share with you is true. The "love letters" were written, the intricate dance of romance unfolded, and lives were changed forever. That's how it began, our mad dash into love and the fires of truth.

And, in the proper fashion of a culture where men are expected to make the first move—he jumped.

SUBJECT: ***That Bloody Australian!***

Hi Kimberley :-)

My name is Adam! I'm not sure what you were told about me, but I'm Australian and currently travelling through South and North America, Canada, Nepal and a bit of Thailand. I've been travelling for about 8 months now…I've met some wonderful people and had some great experiences…I carry a positive attitude everywhere I go (I'm a bit of an extrovert!). I'm also a very straightforward and genuine person.

I am having an amazing experience…such choice and opportunity…I could never have thought that life could be so fantastic! I'm growing in my heart and really know where I am (not literally…lol) but emotionally. I am really comfortable in my own skin…having done a lot of exploration with my heart and soul…I would describe myself as spiritual rather than religious…I'm not into organized religion …but everyone has their own path…I'm interested in knowing more about metaphysics; asking some simple questions can lead to a life of profound change. Anyway…that's probably a bit deep…but I'm sure you won't mind my "prattle"…:-)

I guess you might want to know what I did before leaving Australia. In short, I was a senior policy analyst working in public policy areas such as national security, counter-terrorism, disaster management, and a host of strategic issues…but this is indeed in the past, as I don't seem to fit that life anymore.

I'd love to hear from you…if you would like…I'm currently hiking parts of Glacier and Jasper National Parks…this is fantastic country!!! Not seen any bears yet…so my strategy for not being eaten…is working!

Adam :)

PS. Thank you for the photo, which was sent on to me…you seem lovely…and very pretty :-)…that's a bit flirty!!!…but in my defense it's true! :-)

When I received Adam's first email I was delighted. Okay, I was really knock-my-socks-off impressed. He had taken the time to write more than just a few words; in fact, his words demonstrated that he was willing to challenge himself and his life on an emotional and spiritual level. He was a world traveler, and an adventurer. Most importantly he appeared happy with himself. I needed to know that fact more than anything else: that he was happy with himself. As I sat down to respond to him, I made an important decision: to be as open, authentic, and vulnerable as I knew how to be. I wasn't going to play it safe. His first email opened a door within me, a door that allowed the miracles to flow.

SUBJECT: ***To the Australian Who Intrigues Me***

Dear Adam,

I am delighted to get your email, thank you for the time, the considered thoughts, the sharing…well, just thanks. I'll return the favor so here is my first missive to you:

I live on the beach, so as I write to you I will share the ocean breeze and the wave-filled silence with you.

I feel the sincerity of your note and I send my excitement of the possibilities back to you.

I like the idea of writing letters (sans the snail mail and embrace the email).

I'll start by sharing some of the beauty and mystery going on in my life. Between the lines you will find me, my beliefs, my hopes, my strengths, and my weaknesses.

For the last two years, most of my work has been on myself. I wanted to do more with my life and found that in corporate work I had to camouflage parts of me. I wonder how much of that was true for you in your old life?

I am more than a little intuitive and could get away with it because we all have business "hunches." After a while, the "guys" would just look at me and do what I suggested. Doing so saved them money and often helped them through troubled waters. Also in business there are "rules"; not as many for me (as a consultant) as for others, but rules just the same. It was my job to tell the "big boss" the truth about himself and his company. That part was easy: those things, as you well know, are obvious to anyone with the eyes to see and the heart to hear. The hard part is getting the big boss to do the internal work it takes to really change. I believe that nothing changes until you do. Sometimes the head person (usually a man, but sometimes a woman) has the courage to risk real change, and sometimes not. It hurts me to watch companies go down because the head person would not change.

So, about two years ago, after a string of really big successes and enough money in the bank to be safe, I stopped looking for corporate work. Instead I looked into myself to try and determine what was next for me. What did I really want to do now? To determine that, I needed to look deeper into who I wanted to "be" now.

I have been involved in self-growth work for a long time. It is my first and primary commitment every year. Opportunities to grow are the first things that go on my calendar.

I am really emotional, and psychologically healthy, and have a strong spirituality that works for me. I am glad that is true for both of us. And now the proverbial "but"—with as much as I had, I wanted more from life. I wanted a deeper connection with myself. I don't think I knew that when I started this journey, but I know it now. So for two years, working with two mentors, I have been exploring avenues of myself and also my own human capacity, something most don't explore. Anyone can, but most just aren't interested in doing that work, or pursuing the goal it promises.

For me, the goal was the increased freedom that only comes with more responsibility, more joy, more ways to be loving, and increased abundance on every level. The hardest work was intimacy, i.e. being open, tender, vulnerable, knowing, caring, and loving—with myself. In essence, falling in love with myself.

Sounds strange as I write it, but isn't that what self-love is when you seek it consciously, falling deeply in love with yourself? Sure, it means healing the dark, ugly, resistance and hurt, i.e. the shadow self. It meant (and means) for me, forgiving myself for the dark shadow. And here is the kicker: forgiving myself for fearing the light shadow. We all have dark stuff and most of us, who are healthy, know our failings and our weaknesses. We have practice, often a lifetime of practice, of falling down, stumbling over, and sadly trying to hide from, those parts of us. If we are healthy, we have healed much of our dark shadow. And even when old stuff (patterns of behavior) pops up again, we have the skills to elegantly walk through the process of healing more and more of ourselves. But the light shadow: our magnificence, our grace, our magic, our majesty—those are the things we fear the most.

How much can I love? How much can I see, feel, touch, and create with pure will and choice? How high can I fly? These are things that send the bravest of us into hiding. I don't want a life of hiding, I want a life where I risk the greatness within me, and encourage the greatness in you. I want "more of life" and I do not believe we have even begun to touch the greatness each of us is capable of.

So, for me the foundation of greatness, majesty, and magnificence is self-love. Funny that two little words should hold such power.

The product of my self-love is that now I spend most of my time exploring how I can be more loving. There isn't a hole in me that I want to fill with achievements, other people's approval, the love of a good man, or friends who think I am indispensable. No, now I want to love more. It is not that I don't want the others, I do, it is just that I now have something inside of me that makes me smile just because I am alive. The ineffable does not have words, but I hope you can feel the resonance of what I am trying to say.

I so appreciated you jumping in and sharing. Tell me more. Not just of your journey, which I truly want to hear about, but of the deeper you. You said, "I'm growing in my heart and really know where I am (not literally...lol), but emotionally. I am really comfortable in my own skin...having done a lot of exploration with my heart and soul..."

Please tell me more. What have you learned about your heart, your feelings? What is making life so extra-ordinary? Soul work can change us forever. What has changed in you as you discovered a new skin after having shed the old?

I know it is customary to spend time bantering back and forth, saying nothing of real significance. I am so very pleased and impressed that you skipped that part. Thank you...sincerely ...thank you.

I love your picture, your smile, your happiness. If I could just learn to teleport I would sit by the fire with you tonight and look at the stars and listen as you told me of your adventures. BTW, flirt away, that is so much fun. Let's honor each other by speaking the truth and let's have fun getting to know each other. If nothing ever comes of this, then we had the courage to share our true selves and that in my mind is always a treasured thing.

Smiling into your eyes,

Kimberley

When I wrote those words I meant every syllable. I worked for hours on this email so I could honestly share from the very beginning who I was. I was willing to risk being seen in all my power and in all of my fragilities. What I didn't know then was how much I would learn in a very few days. I didn't know how fast I would fall into love, or how deeply Adam would touch me. I didn't know that some of the words I had written in my first missive to Adam would turn out to be untrue. I didn't know. But then, the lessons to come would be well worth the ignorance that preceded them.

Adam answered me within hours. I remember seeing his email in my in box and catching my breath. I thought, "So fast!" He wasn't holding back either.

SUBJECT: **The San Franciscan Who has Caught My Eye!**

Hi Kimberley :-)

Wow!!! What a wonderful way to greet the day! I woke to read your beautiful email and have reread it now a couple of times, and decided to wait so that I can let the words rest with me a while…I have been restraining myself from writing back immediately, but can no longer wait…it's like watching ice cream melt! I'm compelled to write to you! Talk about intriguing! You've got nothing on me baby!! You have intrigued me, more than you know.

I haven't shared this with anyone, but two days ago I hiked to Lake Agnes, about six kilometers above Lake Louise, late in the evening, to sit at the far end of that beautiful lake. I have a habit of having epiphanies, and "a-ha" moments whilst embracing nature...(The odd act of tree hugging also happens :-)...but don't tell anybody). I usually think best when sitting/walking in the rain (love the moody stuff). I love it when the rain hits my face...I feel connected to the space around me...both physically and emotionally...It truly is an amazing feeling and it's at these times when I connect to my heart...like you described, I'm happy...crazy-happy at being alive! No one there, just me.

Anyway, I too have been searching my heart for insights into what true love is, and like you, I now understand that it is right there in ourselves! And I once again come back to my knowing that the song "Do the Hokey-Pokey" is in fact a LIE! Putting your right foot in is NOT what its all about!! Lol...love and love of the Self is where it's at!

Seriously though...after all, as I am connected to everyone and everything, my "self-love" is really a deep love of the universe and everything in it, including my connection to everything...Unity! I read it in so many of the books I've read over the past couple of years, but only now has it resonated at this deeper level...I'm not denying that my heart is so full of love, and that I want so much to share it with a beautiful feminine heart, because I do...and to deny that is to deny I'm human. And there is nothing quite so beautiful as a feminine heart.

What I thought was love, is not what it turns out to be! There...how's THAT for deep! I had this realization when I was at Lake Agnes and I sort of felt a huge release (almost felt like a cog had shifted gears in me) and smiled at myself because the answer I have been seeking for the last two years had only been obscured by my own belief systems, worn like a coat from my childhood! So I guess what I'm trying to say is, I completely understand where you are coming from, and yes...I deeply resonated with your words and I guess you can tell I am excited by them and the feelings they convey.

The "Soul work" you talk of is definitely what I have been connecting with and I'm very much a changed man from the one with expensive suits, cars, investment properties and a stressful occupation…I jumped off that hamster wheel and now I've have embraced happiness! Which is totally awesome!

I would love to meet you too because I'm sure we have a connection…just not sure what it is yet…and like you mentioned, even if this connection is not of the heart, we will have passed this way for a reason…I guess you can tell that I don't believe in mistakes, only meaningful experiences…we learn from everything. We live in a synchronous world…and thank God!

Hey, whilst I can go deep in my heart space, I can also be fun, with a kooky sense of humor! I can tell you a bit more about me…I love most music…tried opera…and can't get that…sorry …tried…but everything else, is good…but my favorites are acoustic, singer/songwriters, and "alternative" (i.e. not mainstream), I love all food…love the taste, texture, and magnificence of food…I love to eat slowly…with company…I recharge with other people. I don't smoke and only drink an occasional red wine…lately loving Argentinean Malbecs…I also don't gamble and don't take prescription or non-prescription drugs… preferring natural therapies…I love organic anything, and food made with love…I love to hug…I'm a big hugger! And very tactile…arghhh such a revealing man…I'll lose my intrigue…and you won't want to write to me anymore!

Haha…well, I have to leave this little Hostel in Golden and head up towards Jasper…I'll get some hikes in…not sure about internet connectivity in bear-country…so if I'm offline for a while…I'll apologize in advance :-)

I'll sign off now, and get myself organized...I hope you have a great day and I will send you love and light. :-)

Adam

When I read Adam's missive over again, the following words stopped me cold: "the last two years had only been obscured by my own belief systems, worn like a coat from my childhood!"

They stopped me in my tracks because they revealed a profound truth. I have spent the last fifteen years teaching people how to change their beliefs so they can have anything they want in their lives. We create our lives based on how our subconscious mind is hot-wired. The wiring comes in the form of beliefs. I recognized the truth in his words because I lived that truth and studied it. I know that most of our beliefs are formed in childhood. And there it was, all I had learned from literally hundreds of hours of study and thousands of hours teaching in one sentence.

Could Adam really understand the function of the subconscious mind, where beliefs are stored and then played out in our lives? Had I created a man who took responsibility for his own growth? Had I created one who understood himself so well?

I read and reread his email trying to ferret out every nuance of who he might be. I tried, as I had asked him to do, to read between the lines. Was this man real? Think about it. I reread his first two missives. What would you have felt or done if a man or woman wrote those words to you?

What would you do if a potential mate wrote to you with the candor of my first missive to Adam? Most of us say we want love, but, when it is offered as a possibility we all "wear the coats of childhood" and respond in whatever way that demands.

This book is a true love story. A love story that changed and changed again as we challenged our beliefs about love, men, women, trust, and relationships. We had to navigate our thoughts and our doubts about feeling good enough to be loved. We had to climb the steep mountains and jump ravines based on our enduring beliefs about love, and most of all, our beliefs about ourselves.

This book holds the secret to permanent change. We can change anything we want to change in our lives, by learning how to change our beliefs. The first secret is that we must be willing to change. Many of us say we do, but we really do not. Adam and I both had to face profound and permanent change. We had to answer the question for ourselves as individuals, and as lovers: were we willing to change? Was love a big enough reward to risk change?

CHAPTER TWO:

22 Hrs, 6 Mins

WE ALL HAVE the love life we really want. We can scream, curse, jump up and down, get drunk, hurt others, stop feeling, throw this book across the room, but that does not make my words any less true. We all have the love life we really want.

That was true for Adam and true for me. This time we both wanted something more than we had been able to create in the past. To make this possible, this time we had to be willing to dig to the core of our personal beliefs, take ownership of them and intentionally change those beliefs that—while anchored in our pasts—were no longer viable in our present, and most importantly in our futures. In consequence, we were able to change our destinies.

SUBJECT: ***The Man Who is Astounding Me Just by Being Himself***

Hello Adam,

You are out in the wild blue communing with nature as I write this missive. Language is so powerful that I like using words that say what I mean...not just to make noise. A missive is so much more vulnerable than a note, email, message, etc. I like the word and it is joy-filled to share myself with you.

You said such wonderful things and I want to comment and explore some of them more.

Firstly, I just want to say "wow" back at you. Our communication is rare and intimate...a revealing, an unveiling, it makes my heart sing to have the opportunity to share with you. You spoke of the feminine heart and I agree it can change you, anchor you in stormy weather, and lift you to be more than you imagined. It can fill you with love, long awaited. The masculine heart is every bit as magical. It protects and defends. It challenges and inquires. It fills you with love, long awaited. Together they create a sacred spiral, each giving and receiving.

We don't know how we will walk this path: as friends, as lovers, as "the love of our lives," as wise-ones whose touch can last forever...wherever this journey leads us...thanks for sharing it with me.

I love your words...in nature you find epiphanies. "Habit of epiphanies"...such an oxymoron. Few are blessed with true epiphanies...even fewer with more than one. What rare blessings you allow. I believe we create our own realities—all of it. We don't always know why we created or allowed something, but the power is clearly ours. Adam, for you to allow, to receive, to recognize and then contemplate your epiphanies... well, I don't think you understand what an exceptional human being allows all of these.

I know the next is tangential, but this is a missive so I am allowed. :)

There is something sacred about solitude. For me, time alone is necessary. I celebrate with you the quiet moments, where silence is loud in your head, where time doesn't exist and space collapses on itself…coming back to yourself and the world is different.

I love the rain, fog, cold wind, crashing waves, small cabins, fireplaces with endless wood supplies. (I can handle a chainsaw with the best of them, but it's so much more fun if the wood just appears from the back of someone else's truck). Yes, I own a truck, a 1969, ¾-ton Jimmy. I have a mountain home in the middle of the Tehachapi mountain range. Bears, mountain lions, bobcats, deer and golden eagles are my neighbors. Once I was the only living soul with two legs on the mountain. I am sorry to report there are two others now. Not close but still, when I first bought the virgin land I was told not to. No one, most especially not a woman, had ever lived on the land. There is something very special about being the first to be the guardian of the land. I call her Harmony and this is a place where nature loves herself. If I can figure out how to attach a picture I will. More on Harmony, if you are interested, another time.

You say, "And there is nothing quite so beautiful as a feminine heart…" I've been thinking about this, on and off again all day. I decided I would share with you as bravely as you shared with me. Sometimes I ache from wanting a man to love "flat out." Until now, I don't think I was brave enough to love so completely. Oh, I said I wanted to…but there it is again, I create my own reality and if I didn't create a relationship where loving "flat out" was safe, then the truth must be I did not want to. The great thing about loving myself is that a relationship is an option, not a necessity. I am happy and that happiness often elevates to joy, yet when all is said and done, I want to love someone. I want to have a man to gift with my love. How fun, how terrifying all in the same breath. Oh, love is not the only thing that is terrifying, no it is the intimacy, the openness, the vulnerability, the unveiling, that is even more frightening than love.

Somehow it just doesn't seem as frightening any more. Maybe because I know how to recover from hurt, maybe because it is a risk well worth taking, maybe because I trust myself more, maybe all of these and more.

You awed me when you said, "I smiled at myself because the answer I have been seeking for the last two years had only been obscured by my own belief systems, worn like a coat from my childhood!" Again I am astounded that you know this, and more, are living it. Thank you for sharing something so very private and so very precious. I love it that you share from the depths of you. It gives me hope that you really want me to do the same.

I agree we are in sync; there are no coincidences, just synchronicities. Maybe I'll call you "Sync" in honor of these magical moments we are creating. :)

I love that you are a toucher. My thought: Thank the Goddess for that!

You jest when you say, "I am very tactile…arghhh such a revealing man…I'll lose my intrigue!! Lol…and you won't want to write to me anymore! :-)" Nope, good try, but still intrigued and now fascinated with your sensuality. I feel it between the lines and in the flavor of the food you choose, and in the texture of your palms, the pulse on your wrist and the sensitivity of your fingertips.

Did you feel me today? I came to you in meditation. I sat with you once and sent a breeze to caress you another time.

As the jewels of the city lights flicker, I think of stars, trails of quiet solitude and the wonder of your sharing.

'Night

Kimberley

You might wonder how long it took Adam and me to get to this point in our missives to each other. The answer may surprise you, 22 hours and 6 minutes. I went back and checked. We both jumped in heart first. I have never understood why anyone would wait and not dare love when the possibility was right there. Well that is not totally true; I know it is because we are so very afraid. I was tired of being afraid.

Aren't you? As women, as men, what are we waiting for? Jump into the adventure of discovering the other person. If you are waiting for a sign from God that you will not be hurt, that it will all work out and no one will ever break your heart again, you will wait until the day you die. There is no guarantee, ever!

Jeff, my friend who sent me the email that started it all, "Kimberley are you interested in meeting a man?…I might have a ringer for you…" meant that he thought he knew of a man who was of a caliber I would appreciate. He did not mean the relationship, if one developed, would be without risk. All relationships come with risk. Most of the risk is within us not the other person. Let me explain. We create our lives moment to moment, based on our belief systems. If we believe that love hurts, then it will. It is that painful and that simple. If we believe that love heals then it will. Deep in our subconscious mind—imagine it as a computer—are stored our beliefs. Our subconscious mind uses those beliefs just as a computer uses its programming. If it is programmed into our computer, it happens. If it is programmed into our subconscious mind, it happens. Beliefs create our love lives. Beliefs create our reality, all of it. Adam and I jumped into our relationship, not blindly, no—we exposed ourselves, and we revealed our vulnerabilities. We revealed who we believed ourselves to be. Most of the time we were right in those self-perceptions, sometimes, well…

SUBJECT: **A Moment**

Good morning Adam. Yes, you are still very intriguing. If I am being totally vulnerable, even more intriguing.

If this catches you before you head out, know I will write more later. I am running for the hotel door to be in my seat for a spiritual retreat this weekend. More on that later.

I am so excited I feel like a kid, let's eat the ice cream and not watch it melt. I love jumping in feet first. We know who we are, now let's find out who the other is.

So quickly: no drugs, smoking, or alcohol. I live in Southern California not San Francisco. I don't know where I am going to live, but I have known for the last few months I am moving. A new adventure is upon me. I am an explorer at heart. I carry home inside of me, so places don't anchor me, they enhance me.

If you have never been to Yosemite, the valley of love and healing with the river of mercy running through it...she changes me every time I visit. I know, from my prospective, how nature calls to me, changes me and makes me weep with the beauty. Let's walk in the rain sometime and if it is right, let's hold hands. I truly have to go and don't want to. I want to sit and share with you.

More later.

And yes I understand if you can't get to the web. I, with your permission, will come and visit you in spirit in nature. Watch for me, you will know when I am there.

Kimberley

SUBJECT: **A Moment for You**

Hi Kimberley :-)

Oh my lord! I was writing this email (below) to you...and saw/read your lovely email! Wow. You know how to touch a man's heart! You melted me! I agree about the written word, so I will share with you my fantasy...which is, quite simply, to share a transcendent relationship in love...a heart connection in spirit, mind and body.

Your words about the feminine and masculine heart are not only beautiful prose, but shudder through my being literally, as I know them to be true...you may not realize it, but when you say that we may journey this path as friends, lovers, "the loves of our lives" or ones that can touch a life forever...I think you're closer to the last possibility than you know...I'm just overjoyed that there are women like you on this planet...and I'm not just saying that!

And the other possibilities? Well...I'm just excitedly holding my breath...:-)

Oooooh and yes, I felt you at 11:47 a.m., local Alberta time today :-)))) I was tuning in to a beautiful feeling...and there you were! I checked the time, so I know exactly when it was...it may be just in my head...and the timing might be out...but I felt you in my heart! How does a woman do that after a couple of emails?

And and and...your house (Harmony) looks amazing! I'm with you, moody weather, fireplaces, and snuggling up on a couch with a good book and...well...just snuggling :-) I bet you find solace there?

I'm a bit of a traveler! I just pulled into Jasper...and will be bunking in the car tonight...this place is fully booked and it's too dark to set up my tent! I had a great hike into Larch Valley and Valley of the Ten Peaks near Moraine Lake... have lots of photos

...but haven't uploaded them yet...an intriguing hobo! At least I'll have lots of stories to tell you! :-)

You think you're a kid? I get excited to see an email from you...and yes, let's eat the ice cream! It could be fun...and I would love to hold your hand :-) and and and...I'd also love to meet you, but think that is a way off at the moment...due to our distance apart...I have spent 90 days in the US already this trip, so I could not get a visa...even though I would want to...I must leave the continent before returning.

I am aligned with your thinking on where "Home" is. For me, my home is beside the woman I love, not a building or a geographical place...her heart is precious and so that's where I am.

Thank you for sharing about your feelings of vulnerability...please know that I am a safe place...and I totally understand where you are coming from...even though I haven't met you, I feel similar. It is super-unusual for me, but I feel a connection, which I don't understand yet...so I do feel vulnerable...So we can be vulnerable together!

Aaaannnnyyyywwwaaayyy ...

I also wanted to let you know that my commitments from here (Canada) are to go to Nepal on 2 October to undertake a volunteering project for three months teaching English to Buddhist Monks aged 7-12 years. It will be in a monastery just outside Kathmandu. Then I'm heading to Thailand for a week or so...which takes me into mid-January...then...well...I have no plans...and have not made any...and I'm not entirely sure why?

Can you tell me a little about the spiritual retreat you are at? If you are at Esalen, I'm guessing that web access is a bit difficult...actually most places will probably be a bit tough.

I have been to Yosemite...though not for as long as I would have liked...and yes, you're right...it is a very beautiful place...I saw the Giant Sequoias...just in awe of nature :-) Your description of the beach sounds wonderful...I know the sound and feelings you describe ...

Ok...my "other" details are...I'm 6'3" (191 cms) and average build, not into beards...tried that...I have a scar on my tummy from a surgery when I was eight (appendix), I haven't got any tattoos, though I'm not against them...or piercings if they're done tastefully...some can be very attractive on women.

As I write this, borrowing the free WiFi in a hotel car park (no...I'm not kidding!!) I realize you are probably asleep, as this is what most people are doing now...not staking out a hotel car park in Jasper!

Sleep well...I will be thinking of you.

Adam :-)

PS...is it too early to send you a hug?

Looking back now, I think I started falling in love with Adam when he wrote, "I am aligned with your thinking on where 'Home' is...for me, my home is beside the woman I love, not a building or a geographical place...her heart is precious and so that's where I am...thank you for sharing about your feelings of vulnerability...please know that I am a safe place...and I totally understand where you are coming from...even though I haven't met you, I feel similar. It is super-unusual for me, but I feel a connection, which I don't understand yet...so I do feel vulnerable...so we can be vulnerable together!"

Then, rather than just speak about being vulnerable, he moved us to a whole new level.

SUBJECT: ***State of the Heart***

Hi Kimberley,

Just wanted to reach out to you about the vulnerability we share. I don't think either of us could truly understand the hurts that we have had in the past.

But, I feel it is a good idea to let you know, I was betrayed and my heart suffered terribly. It has been two years now and a lot of forgiveness and love has brought me to a place of peace.

I am usually pretty reserved and don't play with other's hearts... I believe strongly in boundaries (I have done a lot of 5th chakra work) and personal will. I respect mine and those of others.

So, all that said, I really appreciate you sharing with me the way you have...and it has made me feel that I can also share with you :-) I know how much a betrayal can hurt, how expectations can be set, and our hearts exposed to the vagaries of life.

Like you, I am resilient and know how to heal...even though such a process is painful...it is from the darkest places where the greatest learning springs...I give grace and blessings to my ex, as I could never be where I am today without her...in the long run...what she has done is awesome!

So...back to vulnerability...yes, it has taken me a while to put my heart back "out there," but I am ready...and I have so much love to give :-) I will do so with "gusto" or...and I like your term..."flat out," for where there is fear (and vulnerability) there is no love...and that's the rub! It's my choice...and I choose love...:-) that raw, naked masculine heart is out there! Protecting and defending!

That's my little "missive" to you :-)

Adam :-)

When I read Adam's missive to me I felt honored and somehow reassured. Adam had suffered and moved beyond the betrayal of his wife. I did not know the story then and did not need to. What I saw and felt was that he had moved beyond it. In my hope, in my budding love, what I missed was that Adam truly felt that, "It is from the darkest places where the greatest learning springs." That should have scared me because too many of us have that as a belief. If we believe growth comes from pain then if we strive to grow, if we want more from life, we must create dark places from which we can emerge more whole.

I am the first to say it is not smart to fall in love with love letters. It is a mistake, one I had made in the past, so this time I knew better. I also knew that chemistry cannot be manufactured no matter how much I might want it to be between me and a man. If it is not there in the beginning, it is rare for it to develop later in the relationship. I had made that mistake before as well. So this time I wasn't going to do either.

I could feel myself opening more and more to Adam, and his latest missive told me the same was true for him. When he said he was leaving for a prior commitment in Nepal and that we would not be able to meet until January, I rebelled. No way was I accepting that reality. So I acted, and our first miracle happened.

SUBJECT: ***I Need You to do Something for Me***

> *Oh Adam, you touch me so very deeply. I don't know why your email didn't get to me last night. (I received both this morning.) They are so beautiful and I would have never left you hanging wondering what I was thinking and feeling after you shared from the depth of you. What I think and feel is moving faster than I would have dreamt. Was it only Thursday that we said '"hi"? There is no time or space and I am trying to remember that and not boundary us by what should be, rather what we want to create together.*

I am so glad you felt me. I felt you this morning. It was as if you were standing right there looking down at me as I was sitting in my chair. I did not take a watch into the session so I don't know exactly what time, but I saw and felt you. Thanks for the touch.

There is something very important on my mind. NO, please don't go to Nepal until we have at least shared even 10 minutes in person. Of course, I want you to go and follow all of your dreams, but first I want us to meet.

Here is why: I am getting in pretty deep here, way too fast for common sense. But I am not common, nor thank the stars, are you. So I really want to know if there is chemistry between us. I know that is really, really forward and I would have let it rest, but you are leaving until after the holidays. Yes go…explore…be free to be you…but please let's at least figure out how to touch once before you go.

Are you willing? Please be willing. We can easily figure out where and when.

Kimberley

PS: I want to write you about your missive and I will tonight, but I am on a lunch break and I needed to ask you if we could meet before I go back into the session, otherwise I would be talking to you in my heart and not paying attention.

More later.

Seventeen minutes later the answer came.

SUBJECT: **Re: I Need You to do Something for Me**

I just got back from hiking the Whistlers summit trail here in Jasper…a short hike…but beautiful nonetheless…when I was there I was talking to my hiking mate Shirley (I've told her all about you) and and and I told her that I wanted to meet you :-)

So…

Yes, yes, yes…I want to meet you too…arghhh I thought it might be too early to ask, so I didn't…the chemistry thing is really important.

As I wrote, but have yet to send, I have discerned that you are a beautiful soul, who I would really like to get to know…you are someone who is as passionate about the human condition as I am, isn't afraid of talking about her feelings nor hearing about mine, wouldn't be afraid to call me on stuff, is confident (and probably feisty! :-), is in a good place within herself emotionally and spiritually…and someone I have a connection with.

I'm standing in the bookshop aisle, looking at "The Book of Kimberley," and I've only read the first page, but I'm so interested in what happens next…my heart is beating faster, I no longer care what the shop owner thinks of my prolonged stay in the shop…I'm here, now…with this book…It feels wonderful in my hands and I cradle it carefully, it smells wonderful (I love the smell of books by the way). I've decided, I'm going to read it…it's more than curiosity now, the story intrigues me and I somehow know that there is a message here for me…an important one…my heart tells me so.

So, yes, please let's meet…and if things don't pan out, then at least we can be mates. Though I'm not sure I can get into the States…I can go into the embassy here to see if I can come to see you…OMG…I'm like a teenager…again!

Let me know what you think…I am driving towards Penticton tonight to arrive tomorrow afternoon…I will have connectivity tonight about 8:00 p.m. here or 7:00 p.m. in California.

Adam

Emails flew back and forth only minutes apart. How did lovers survive the wait days or weeks for snail mail to reach them—or months for boat mail? We were blessed mere minutes for our hearts to sing.

SUBJECT: **Re: I Need You to do Something for Me**

I am so happy. You have no idea. And yes we will be mates, but more than mates. There is something between friends and lovers, and that is endearingly committed friends.

I am hoping for the more, but you are so precious to me already, let's shoot for the star. OMG I am so excited. If you cannot get here I will come to you. Ok, I am back into the workshop. It is not too early for a hug, one that blends us until we are one. I love hugs where you lose the boundaries and meld.

Just to be clear my vote is for lovers. Wow, talk about vulnerable.

Kimberley

SUBJECT: **Re: I Need You to do Something for Me**

Haha...yay!! I vote for lovers too :-)

And and and...I'm soooo glad you like hugs! I like the sound of a melding hug...you will have to teach me!

I hope we like each other when we meet...I'm anxious now...arghhh...I also have something to tell you (below) and it may influence your decision to meet with me...But I wanted you to know.

A question ...

I have read your corporate website, which gives me a sense of the business persona, But I don't have a website and apart from our emails and my Facebook, (oh...and of course my assertions that I'm an awesome guy!) how do you know you want to meet with me?

For me, it's a sense I have in my body…my heart is really urging me…my intuition is clear, I'm breathing clear air…and everything tells me this is exactly the way it's supposed to be…and it makes my heart joyous…because I've never had this feeling before…where everything has lined up and then there's something else…and it has freaked me out.

I can share with you…though I'm not sure how you'll take it…but in the interests of full disclosure I believe it's better to have all the cards on the table. I cannot say whether it's true or not, and I'm not sure you are the one who is referred to in this story… (talk about super vulnerable)!!! Geeez…what am I doing?

So, please take it for what it is.

On May 10 this year, during my volunteering project, I was sleeping in my bed in Cusco, Peru. I had meditated the night before (mostly seeking insights into death…a bit morbid…but work with me :-)

Anyway, I asked many questions of my higher self…I slept really well and just when I was waking up the next morning, before my eyes opened and the feet hit the floor, I had this really weird conversation with myself…but ostensibly it was about Walt Disney…I know, right? Weird!

I was wondering about his cryogenic quest…in the context of death and the soul…and then asked a question…in my head…It was "I wonder if I will ever get to meet him?" Then this is where it gets weird…I heard an answer!

It was deep in my mind…but I heard it as clear as a bell…(my friend Sandy in Australia will back me up on this) the answer was "After Kim!" OMG!

I have never heard voices before or since…I had the highest security clearance in Government and underwent extensive psych tests and countless mandatory re-evaluations…I know I'm not crazy.

So, when Jeff sent me your email address and said you would be interested in chatting to me, my heart skipped more than one beat! I don't know who or what Kim is…but you are the first Kim I've had contact with…and our connection is pretty amazing.

Soooooo…you probably think I'm a bit crazy now…so if you'd prefer not to meet, then I'll understand…but I have this integrity thing going on…it's one of my top values, and I believe, it's good for you to know…plus, secrets don't make for lasting connections.

Just in case you still want to meet, I'm heading back to Burnaby early so I can give myself enough time to do the things that need doing for me to see you. Arghhh, I'm extra anxious now! And vulnerable. Like you wouldn't believe.

At least know that I'm sincere when I recount this story…I won't deny it…it sounds amazing, but when I learned of your name I was very taken aback…and though it has not influenced me in chatting to you (like a self-fulfilling prophecy), I have been mindful of it…and given we are planning to meet, I wanted you to know.

I soooo hope you still want to meet…I'm desperate to find out what a melding hug feels like!

Adam :-)

SUBJECT: **Re: I Need You to do Something for Me**

Hi Kimberley :-)

I don't know how that happened…but I have 30 days remain-

ing on my current visa…I thought that I could only stay for 90 days…must be a special under the ETSA Visa Waiver Program for Australians…yay!

What this means is that if you would still like to meet, I will jump on a flight to California to meet you!

Though, if you could confirm for me, that this is what you want. Then leave the rest to me, and no judgments if you choose not to. Totally cool.

Adam!

Ooooh I hope you reply soon. My stomach is in knots!

SUBJECT: **YES**

Okay, cut to the chase. YES come.

Okay, no more knots. I am so sorry I was not here to end your suspense. What a long day for you. Of course I want you to come, even more. And in honor of full disclosure. if you hang out with me you will probably have more of those experiences. We, meaning humankind, do not yet have an inkling of how powerful our subconscious and unconscious minds are, but they are beyond powerful. We are all connected, so when we are on our Soul's path things fall into place. Struggle ends, psychic avenues open up and, dear Adam, it has nothing to do with being crazy. It has everything to do with being courageous enough to have doorways open to other levels of understanding. We can talk more about this.

As to 30 more days on your visa, I am just so jazzed, and nervous, and scared, and happy, and confident. Oh, it is just a jumble. I am going to keep writing more but on another email. If you are still up I want you to know right away that you are welcome…in so many ways it is just plain scary.

More coming,

Kimberley

SUBJECT: **YES**

Yay! I'm up…I was waiting for your email…PHEW…I will rest much more easily now…Ahhhh, breathe again :-)

Eeeeeek…now I'm also excited, scared, nervous, happy and confident!

Questions…when would you like me to visit you? And how long do you think I might stay…I will stay in a hotel near you…so if you could recommend something that would be great. Alternatively I can jump on the Internet and see what's there.

Adam :-)))))

SUBJECT: **YES YES YES**

Well I know what happened, in regards to 30 days magically appearing on your visa, we are being blessed. How grand is that! Ok, I can slow down and catch my breath. It was awful knowing you were anxious and I was the cause.

Firstly, I want to honor your integrity. It is so beautiful. So let me answer your question. Why do I want to meet you? Because my heart tells me so. I believe in my heart and I believe in you. You might well ask how do I know. Well, I know beyond time and space. Could I be wrong…sure…but I don't believe I am. What do I lose by being wrong? Absolutely nothing. What can I gain by following my heart and finding out I was correct, that you are the man I believe you to be…the possibilities are endless.

So far, this is what I know about you: I love how you reveal yourself; I think you are great-looking and I love how you dress;

I love your energy; I admire your willingness to explore, most importantly, yourself; and then the world.

I know you have been devastated and used. Your broken heart creating a new space for you to be reborn. You have remade yourself, this time handcrafting the life you want and not one that was picked for you.

I know you are sensuous and long to find someone that matches your desire to be touched, not just in bed, but during the day for "no reason at all." I know you want and have admitted to yourself the need for a special woman who can think as fast as you, keep up with your heart's longing to help the world, make you safe with her loyalty and strength and who allows you to keep her safe and treat her as the precious being you see her to be. I know you are beautiful on the inside and finding out just how beautiful you are is a new revelation for you. I know you want to give more than you want to receive and I might have to wrestle you to the ground to get you to receive all the love you deserve. I know you are gun-shy and I know you have courage. I know your active brain needs to be challenged but more your heart needs someone to love in order to be really happy. I know you could become a master of loving. You pay attention to the details, which is key to really loving someone in the way they need to be loved rather than in the way you want to love. I know you are brave and honest. I know you are tender and kind. I know you can be easily wounded, as can anyone who has decided that living behind shields and masks is not a life worth living. I know that I know nothing yet and want to learn everything you will share.

Okay, so let me catch up with you. I am 5'6" if I stretch my neck, but don't stand on tiptoes. I am in ok shape, not overweight, but could certainly get myself to the weight gym and tone. I have recently redefined a relationship...that sounds weird so let me explain. For the last four years I have been in a relationship with a friend and we never have been able to move it to lovers. We tried because we had so much in common. He was the first man I had been with who no matter what I asked for in regards to him looking at an issue between us, or about himself, that he always, always took the request seriously and explored. That was worth a lot to me, but in retrospect we both made a mistake. There was absolutely no chemistry between us and though we tried, it just never worked. Lots of whys and wherefores, but to make a long story short we were and are much better friends. So there was no huge break-up because we didn't have a lovers' relationship, we had friendship and that will last. We are both so much happier as friends.

I am a tree hugger, have no political affiliations, just the person, and the issues matter to me, collect crystals and believe in their power, and have clear intuition as is true for many of my friends. I hang with people who believe in the same power for goodness as I do and believe we are responsible to birth a new world. I am a metaphysician and most certainly know that there are powers and forces beyond human. No, not aliens that land and want to eat our livers :) but non-physical beings that have come to share if we care to listen. See, that is why your missive about having a vision and hearing a possible connection to my name made me smile rather than scared me. Things like that happen to my friends and myself on a pretty regular basis. (My brothers, both military, think my beliefs are crazy, but love me anyway.)

If none of that has scared you away, please come. I truly want you here and in my life in whatever capacity fits for us both. Our higher selves have worked overtime to help us create this with elegance and ease; I vote we oblige them and ourselves.

Sleep dear Adam, in peace tonight.

Kimberley

Adam and I had created our first miracle. No issues with visas, no resistance to meeting, no pressure, no safety issues. Adam just made it easy. He made sure I felt safe and that we could be crazy-excited together.

We risked from the beginning. We allowed ourselves to be excited and to express it. Our beliefs about the beginning of relationships were in alignment and worked for the two of us. Any resistances that might have been, were cleared out of the way because our beliefs worked for us. In the second half of this book you will find out exactly how that process works. But for now, keep in mind how easily possible obstacles were cleared out of the way. Our subconscious minds are just that powerful. If you do not believe miracles like this are possible, then they will not be for you. We all have the life that our beliefs dictate.

CHAPTER THREE:

5 Days, 1 Hr, 3 Mins

ADAM CHANGED my destiny. I changed his. Love not only tempts fate, it changes fate: not as a predetermined journey upon which you have no say, but rather fate as the path you choose, because of the beliefs you hold.

Remember, I told you I believed everything I wrote to Adam in my first missive to him. I told him I did not need a man in my life to fill me. I was not one of those needy people that need a partner in order to feel whole, or loved. I told him I had no "lack" in myself.[1] He told me he was healed from his relationship from a woman who repeatedly betrayed him. He said he had no issue with self-love or deserving. We were both wrong.

We did not know that in the beginning. We were as open and as honest as we knew how to be. As the days passed, we wrote more and more. Adam created a book, *The Book of Kimberley*, where we could each write something that honored the reality that *we* were the authors of our love story. Back and forth we wrote, each creating our parts of the story. In this way we declared our intention to the universe and to one another.

SUBJECT: **I Am Writing a "Book of Kimberley"**

I am coming to be with you. I have no intention of putting my "Book of Kimberley" down.

I'm just getting to the part where they meet for the first time, he is so anxious to meet her…his heart is in his mouth in anticipation, and she is so lovely…and they already know…but are too afraid to dream.

It's going too fast for both of them…but they are not willing to give up on each other…not yet.

They know this connection is special and so there will be time enough for brakes later…but for now, they are dancing around each other…inquiring, loving, caring, and being…the possibilities are swirling…and endless…what if …

I wonder what's next?

More ham-fisted attempts at prose to come.

Adam

SUBJECT: **Chapter 2 of "The Book of Kimberley"**

Just when she was totally freaking and closing herself down he took her hand and reassured her. He whispered, "It is going to be ok. No matter what happens, I am right here with you." She cried for a moment. It was so strange in her reality to have someone to lean on, if only for a moment. The whisper was enough, the excitement resurfaced and more the wise woman stepped up, reminding her of who she really is…a master magician of the current and coming age.

Remembering and honoring all that she has been taught, she laughed at herself. Spinning with joy, she said to the sky and to the trees, to the light and to the wind, "I create my own reality, all of it. I can use magic to ease our way." So she reached out to the one who caught her just as she was going to fall and said, "Thank you for being you. Thank you for being there when I needed you. I so rarely will admit to needing help. You touched me, Adam. I am ok now. Thank you."

My attempt at prose for you. Now look at the time 2:33 my time. I am sending you the whispers I promised. Feel my gratitude and my soft caress. Feel my caring and my vulnerability.

When I sit still like this and spend time with you in my mind, my heart swells. I imagine you. I imagine us. I imagine. Imagination is the most powerful of all of the creative tools. Expectancy and desire are the others. It is expectancy that usually kicks me in the butt. To keep from being too vulnerable, too exposed we don't reach for what we want with everything that we are. We try to protect ourselves from hurt by limiting how much we will allow ourselves to expect. In Chapter I, in your newly created "Book of Kimberley" you wrote "...and they already know...but are too afraid to dream..." Adam, let's rewrite that. Let risk dreaming. I want to dream with you. I want there to be fantastic chemistry. I want us to lust for each other. I want us to be willing to love each other and to be in love with each other. I want more than I have ever had, to do that I must be courageous. That means being willing to be wrong in pursuit of what right. To charge ahead knowing I don't have all the answers. Dance with me Adam. Take me into you arms and dance with me.

Imagine getting off the plane and seeing me. Imagine your heart rate elevating and your body doing whatever it does when you desire a woman. Imagine me so excited that I can hardly say hello. Imagine that rather than rush into each other arms let's be really vulnerable. Let's reach and touch each other fingertips looking into each other eyes and really seeing. Let's move our hand up and touch palms. Let's feel each other's pulse, let's move our hands up our arms and really experience each other. Let's hug and be one, OR any other way you want me to imagine our first meeting. Tell me what you want and we will do that.

But let's not "wait and see" let's consciously create our reality. For me that means I get to consciously create you being so hot I can't stand it. I don't want or need for you to be perfect. I really, truly don't. I just want you to ache for me and I desperately want to ache for you.

I know this breaks all the rules. Let's rewrite the rules. Ones that create boundaries that work for us. Oh god Adam, let's use magic.

Keep thinking about me. I think about you. But let's elevate thinking to imagination. To work the imagination has to be filled with feelings, intensity and focus. We both know how to do that.

Gratitude begets gratitude...it is a magnet...the more we feel it the more our lives will be overflowing with things to be grateful for...I am so grateful we have given ourselves, with the help of our higher selves, each other.

I am so glad we have this magical opportunity, let's use it wisely.

Hold me in your arms Adam and let's dance.

Kimberley

To you it may seem outrageously sentimental and even adolescent; to us it was a portal of love. We needed an avenue to express our dreams and desires to each other. Adam gave us that portal by creating *The Book of Kimberley*. Together we danced into our deepening relationship in an entirely new way. We reached to each other as we wrote, unveiling ourselves as best we could. We allowed the sentimental, the romance, the anxiety and the support. We were in this together, and together we journeyed.

SUBJECT: ***Trouble***

Good Morning Kimberley!

OMG! I'm in real trouble! I no longer have to imagine you're hot! You truly are a gorgeous woman! Thank you so much for the new photo; you have such a beautiful energy, and your smile is just radiant! This photo has a different feel to your PR shots.

I'm so looking forward to seeing you tomorrow (today)…I'm still nervous and my heart is still aching…and and and…I'm excited…talking with you on the phone helped me breathe again and feel less nervous…but also heightened my anticipation…I just want to be with you.

So…turning the page to the next chapter of my "Book of Kimberley" here is chapter 2.75.

"He dreams of them in the hours before they meet and, at her urging, dares to imagine another life…one that has eluded him for the longest time. She whispers to him, and gently touches his consciousness with reassuring tones…they are together in mind and spirit…their hearts aching for each other, for that gentle touch…his mind races…sensing her warmth, her heart, her scent, her loving caress…the beautiful and precious feminine…the Goddess.

He is barely breathing…he reaches for her in the darkness and finds her…a vision of beauty, her presence teases his desires, she is magical…a transformation…she is transcendent.

As she creates magical chemistry, he is transfixed…his heart is overflowing with love, his mind is still and at peace but his body is raw with hunger to become one…and as the vision slowly recedes to the inner reaches of his consciousness her faint scent lingers…she lives within his heart, sees through his eyes, feels with his skin, and merges with his spirit. A true creation of life and love."

Yep! I told you I can't wait!

I hope you are dreaming and resting…I can feel you…you are so near and yet so far away.

I can sleep on the plane…but the house is now quiet after the mayhem earlier in the night…I will see you in only 19 hours…I'm deep in trouble, and my dissenting voice has not arisen.

I know. I can say "see you soon" and actually mean it!

Adam xoxoxo

SUBJECT: **Soon**

Writing my part in this chapter of "The Book of Kimberley."

"It is too early to be awake, but she slides out of bed to be with the ocean and to call to him. Over the seas, her friend the wind flies to deliver her missive, curves around the San Juan Islands and, ignoring the border guards, makes its way to Vancouver searching for him. He is awake too. Waiting for her to come to him.

The wind whispers, "I am here." He holds up the covers and she slides into his warm embrace. Tucking the covers around them both he holds her. Breathing in her scent, marking his brain with the wonder of his woman. She snuggles into him placing her head on this heart and smiling. "Home," she whispers.

Days of anticipation are over…finally together."

Good morning, Adam.

My stomach is all knotted up and it is hard to catch my breath. You will be coming to me very soon and yet a busy day awaits us both. I know you are up thinking about us. I am so glad you liked the picture and you find me appealing.

Your prose moved me, stirred and rekindled fires put to sleep long ago. I am nervous and excited. No negative ego trying to spread doubt, but he is a sneaky bastard, so I will be extra vigilant today about negative thoughts.

Twelve hours Adam, and we will be stumbling over our tongues searching for the words and finally holding each other. I am so terrified and so excited.

Come Home to me Adam.

Kimberley

SUBJECT: ***Re: Soon***

Good morning Kimberley,

Yes, well…"appealing" is an understatement! "Gorgeous," to me, is an innate beauty, that radiates from the heart…and I can see it in your eyes, and your smile…in your energy… you are also physically beautiful…and I like the term "hot," because that's how I feel when I see you…so, "appealing"… sorry…I'm not letting you get away with that one! :-)…just sayin'!

During my last days in Seattle, Washington, I wrote in my journal about what I desired in my woman…what I found attractive and would "push my buttons" when I met her, so that when we met I would know it was her…and they were: love, grace, honor, integrity, and a spiritual heart, ready to create and welcome change.

I'm soooo excited, because when I said you touched my soul, what I was actually saying was that you have all of these intrinsic qualities and it is rare to find such an extraordinary woman. The manner of our meeting will be making our higher selves jump and give each other "high fives" at their own brilliance!

I also wrote at the very bottom of the page (with a smiley face next to it)…"I'm coming to get you"…not in a menacing way…but that I'm coming, please hold on.

I feel I am truly blessed to be sharing your space and have slept my night in gratitude at how wonderful this all is…I don't know how to astral travel, but if I did, with your permission, I would have come to visit you last night and held you in my arms. My tummy is also doing somersaults…I can't think of anything other than seeing you.

Yes, Kimberley…I'm coming for you…and I'm never going to be the same…already you have shown me my masculine and loving heart in a way I've not experienced before…through our missives to each other…and you've given me a glimpse at the power of our co-creation. I am humbled. Thank you! I am falling into you.

Keep that sneaky bastard, your negative ego, at bay! You will find my heart open and ready for you…to protect and defend…I'm sure my heart field is bigger than this house I'm in…it needs a home! All this aching is making me think I'm having a heart attack…it's a physical ache…:-) arghhh…Lol.

Today!

Adam :-))) xoxo

The day had arrived. Just six days from when we first wrote hello. We were both scared out of our shoes. Even with cell phones, it took forty minutes of a comedy of errors to find each other in Los

Angeles airport. But, then he was there, and even though we had spoken about taking it slow we threw ourselves into each other's arms. No hesitation, no real thought, it was just right. The embrace worked, the kiss worked, the chemistry was there. We both sighed with relief and laughed at ourselves. Finally, it only took our entire lifetimes and six calendar days, but we found one another. And we did not rest on the seventh day!

We had survived the second hurdle: chemistry. The first was our willingness to be intimate with each other. That hurdle we had jumped with apparent ease. So together we settled into discovering what it was like to be in each other's presence. For me it was wonderful. Adam communicated with his touch, as well as his words. He challenged each of us to stay totally honest. He got angry when I did something he thought was out of sync with our relationship or integrity. He was vulnerable and strong. He was everything I had asked for in a man.

His words lead me to believe he felt the same. He wrote love missives to me, "It's not hard for me to imagine what I feel like when I desire a woman...I have this feeling when I read your missives and imagine you writing them...but my desire goes more deeply than the physical...I'm getting lost in you, your heart, and I sense you everywhere...you are touching some very deep parts of my soul, my heart also is swelling with love...I'm past aching...(although this feeling is now constant). I've reached some new place...one I've never known.

My usual defenses are not there (that voice is silent...you know the one that says "she's not right for you," with a veritable cast of reasons). I want so desperately to dance with you, to create magic and a wild chemistry, along with a new reality...I want to smell your scent, to taste your sweat, and feel your skin with mine...to touch and hold your hands, and feel your forearms... and hold you...so yes, I can describe what it feels like when I desire a woman, but you are not just "a woman," you are much more. I am very passionate in love, and in life...I am awake! And seeing you."

The very few days we had before Adam had to leave for Kathmandu were filled with words of love, patient acceptance of each other's humanness and turbulent times of "sitting in the fire."

One of Adam's most important criteria for a partner in his life was having a woman who could sit with him in what he called "the fire." A woman who could deal with the issues that always arise in relationships, by sitting with him, touching in some way, and diving into the issue. He was looking for a woman who could express herself even when angry, live within the boundaries of fair fighting rules and stay until the issue was resolved. He found that woman in me.

For myself, it was the first time in my life when I was not the only person in the relationship who said, "We need to talk." It was a delight and a challenge. Someone called me on my stuff. Without harm, he held me accountable to myself, to him, and to the relationship.

In our first hours together I told Adam everything I had not yet shared. He had never asked my age and I deliberately did not tell him. I wanted him to see me, touch me and kiss me before I told him. I knew, for reasons only clear to the gods of intuition, that age was a prejudice of his. So I sent him a current picture and waited. I was delighted when he wrote, "Gorgeous." I told myself that was good enough. It was not.

I thought I was being totally fair when I shared my age with him long before we were sexually intimate, and within hours of our meeting. If he was going to reject me because I was older than him, I wanted him to do that before I fell any deeper in love.

When I told him, we had our first "sitting in the fire." He was angry, really angry. If I had been more aware, I would have known my lie by omission had tapped into his unresolved rage at his dishonest, lying and betraying ex-wife. He told me outright he would not have come if he had known my age. He was angry that I was not as honest as he had been, when he revealed all that might have had me reject him. So we sat in the fire. He was right that I had withheld. I was wrong in doing so. I should have told him and I did not.

The dynamics were not as simple as they appeared. I lied by omission; I did. While I could justify it by saying, "See, you wouldn't have come, and look at all we would have missed." But that was (and is) just crap. I lied and he had a right to be angry.

It was not that he didn't think I was beautiful, appealing, and in his own words, "A gift from the Goddess herself." No, that was not the issue. I was everything he ever wanted in a woman.

Did Adam leave? No. Did he decide on friendship? No. He stayed and began to work through his fear of being with another woman who would lie and betray. That was his real fear. Not my age, but that I had not told him my age. Age was simply the hook he hung his fear upon.

I was wrong, and had justified the withholding in my mind. In my fear, I had acted irresponsibly and that was simply not acceptable to me. So I went to work to discover the belief I had to have that jeopardized our love. I discovered that I withheld because I did not feel that I was enough, because of my age. After all I was twelve years older than Adam. I had my own age prejudice I had never faced. I had to search my fears and my own belief of being not enough.

By the time I intuited that age might be an issue, I was already so emotionally involved that I refused to risk losing him. If he had asked, I would have told him the truth, but he didn't. I used his not asking as my excuse. Our unresolved beliefs around love hit us both in the face on our very first day together. I had a belief that I was not good enough to love so he would ultimately reject me. By being older than Adam, I was not perfect for him. My underlying belief was that I was not enough for him.

Adam had a belief that he did not deserve to be loved. If Adam could find something about me, anything at all that proved that women could not be trusted, then he could justify his most prevalent underlying belief, that he doesn't deserve to be loved.

Kimberley's beliefs:
If I am not perfect I will be rejected.
If I am not perfect I will not be loved.
No man will love me the way I want to be loved.

Adam's beliefs:
Women cannot be trusted.
I don't deserve to be loved.
I am not enough.

How in the world did we discover which beliefs were in our way? The second part of this book, *The Story of Change*, is about just that: learning. Part Two teaches you—step by step—how to uncover your personal beliefs, and how to use the Change Process and your inner strength to change them. In the second half of this book you will find many secrets to the parts of your life that do not work. You will discover the beliefs that form your reality, and then how to consciously change them. And…as highlighted earlier, the most powerful learning will take place if you don't skip ahead to Part Two. You will need the examples from Part One to help you with your self-examination, which will lay the groundwork to the changes you choose to create in your belief systems, and therefore your future.

Personal reflection leading to changes in beliefs is a life-long journey. In Part Two, you will learn techniques to change beliefs. I have been working on changing beliefs that no longer work for me for a long time and, as I explained above, a discordant belief still knocks me on my butt from time to time.

The good news is I know how to change them, once I discover that they are not working for me. Consequently, I can literally change myself in a matter of hours. This is not the hyperbole or psychobabble you read in quick fix, self-help books. No, this is a journey into your subconscious mind and once you develop the skill you can change yourself, truly change yourself, within a few hours.

Knowing how to discover the beliefs that don't work for you, and learning how to change them, is one of the most important skills you can learn to create the life you have dreamt of having. Adam and I continued our journey together. His bountiful gift of love changed me. It shone from him like a beacon of radiant light. When I was ready, we shared our bodies as well as our hearts. In this too he was an amazingly skilled and giving partner. By the time the clock ran out and he had to head to Kathmandu, we were planning our life together.

CHAPTER FOUR:

8 Days, 12 Hrs, 1 Min

THE TIME had come. Adam and I stood in each other's arms looking over the ocean. We had to part for a few months, a short time in the history of one's life, but it felt like a yawning void in my heart. We reassured one another with plans of our future. We made plans for Adam to come back to the US, and home to me. We had spoken of him getting a job that honored his desire to work with teens that needed the guidance and love of a good man. The details, I knew, we could handle. The parting we could weather as well.

As I pulled up to the international terminal at LAX, I stopped and looked out through the windshield for a moment, seeing nothing. Adam reached over and touched me, and I smiled for him. I climbed out of the car with much more spirit than I felt. I did not want to send him off with tears. I wanted him to enjoy his adventure. And I wanted him to come back home to me.

We stood on the bustling sidewalk in each other's arms as people brushed by. We kissed, the way lovers do, with longing and promises. Then, too soon, Adam threw his rucksack over his back and walked through the doors. Through the automatic glass doors he walked, and then stopped and looked back. Again, I smiled for him. I really wanted to run and hold him one more time. I wish now that I had.

As I pulled away from the curb, he was still standing on the other side of the glass looking at me. I waved again and had an awful feeling that I would not see him again. I almost stopped the car to run back to tell him of the heart-breaking premonition I had just had. Again, I wish I had.

Instead, I went back home and crawled back into the bed we had so recently shared, and wrote to him.

SUBJECT: ***I Ache for You***

Dearest Adam,

On the way home my body physically started to ache for you. I just hurt. Yet, I want you to go on your adventure; it is really important that you do. So don't take anything I say as a back-handed request for you to stay. I just want you to know how much you mean to me. I am home and back in bed, so I can smell you for a while longer. You will pick this missive up when you land in Seattle, and know I am thinking and feeling for and about you!

Travel with my love surrounding you and in your heart.

Much, much love, K.

SUBJECT: **RE: *I Ache for You, Gate 69B***

Hi gorgeous! It seems we are very much in synch…I wrote the following at LAX. Gate 69B

Arghh! After the turmoil of LAX security and TSA, I had a chance to catch my breath…and the yawning hole I already feel at our parting is eating me…I'm in a mixed state of tiredness, longing, and that bloody aching in my heart is back! What have you done to me, my love?

Thank you for everything you have done and said for and to me over the last week…I treasure it ALL! I am truly blessed to have you in my life, touching me the way you do…in my heart, soul and my body…you are a beautiful woman in every degree!

You have touched my life on this planet in a way that no other human has ever done…to convey "what you mean to me" cannot be neatly wrapped up in a song, and to be perfectly honest, I'm still not sure of the depth of my feelings for you…they have surpassed any relationship I've ever had (except for my children)…and and and…in eight days! OMG!

It will take some time for me to begin to grasp how much you mean to me…you are in my heart, and yes, your love surrounds me and nurtures my Soul…I will email you again tonight with the number of the place I'm staying…it will be lovely to hear your voice again.

"A backhanded request" I know you better than that Kimberley! I love your straight talking and I know that if you wanted me to stay you would have come right out and asked! Though, as you know, this is a commitment I have made and I agreed with you that my going was important…I have work to do, and need space to do it in…but you will always be there…in my heart, with me as I confront my own issues around love, shame and deservability…I am good enough…I just need to believe it!

I will talk to you soon …

Adam xoxoxoxoxo

I was not the only one in the light and heat of newborn love wrestling with beliefs that did not work. Adam, during our time together stumbled upon his beliefs around being good enough for me. He worried about starting a new career and the economic difference this would make in our circumstance. In his old role as a security adviser for his country, he did not work on knowing himself in the way he had been doing during his trek around the world. He feared I was "ahead" of him in my development. As often as I reassured him he had to face that demon himself, my comfort was in the fact that he was willing to do so.

I might have been more concerned about the economic difference, if Adam's innate wisdom was not every bit as prevalent as mine. No, I was more concerned about the still festering issue around withholding my age.

Adam wrote:

SUBJECT: **It's Me!**

> *I have you in my heart and my soul…*
>
> *I have been thinking about what you wrote and feeling its resonance within me…and what it all means…I am a happy man, you have made me happy!*
>
> *Getting truly in touch with my authentic self is a new experience…all of your "what ifs" sparked the same feelings for me…arghhh…my vulnerability towards you, and any humiliation I might feel, should we decide to end us, will be swamped by my own learning and gratitude for your grace and love you have shown me. I am open to you, as you are open to me…this is not a one-way feeling…we are a musical instrument that, when all strings are tuned, makes beautiful music…but if either one is "off" for any reason, the notes are sour.*
>
> *I am committed to walking with you on this path, hand in hand…we have uncovered some learning for each other, and my*

lust for true understanding of what you mean to me, including what bags reside under my bed and, with help, examining each one, is an exciting prospect…and I am willing to go for as long as it takes. So that when I speak, I come from a place of knowing …

The process to get to that point scares me beyond measure. What ugliness about myself…what vanity…what superficiality will I uncover?…I know it's there…it's like putting your hand down a sewer…uncomfortable, smelly, and gagging…but at the same time rewarding, cleansing and ABSOLUTELY NECESSARY!

But please know, I am coming from a place of love and compassion and will gently work through everything I can, so that our music…should we choose to play…will always be a delight!

I did have a thought about your decision to not tell me your age before I came to meet you, noting it was great in the long term, to avoid my prejudice as you did…but I would have liked to have made that decision, as it was mine to make…it is important to begin with trust and love, for without this, a cancer will erode us.

I will write soon…rest with my comfort, love and blessings surrounding you…as I know you are with me.

Adam xoxoxo

On Day nine I was just beginning to understand the gravity of my lie, of my withholding. I responded with candor.

SUBJECT: ***It's Me! And I am so Glad it is.***

Hi Me,

It was and is your decision to make. I have thought about it and whether I would have done it differently. I don't think so Adam. I think I would still wait for you to see me, so that there was a possibility for us. That is as honest as it gets. I know, given the betrayals in your life that this could balloon into an issue of ongoing trust. But to lie to you now, and tell you I would do it differently would be the ultimate dishonor to what we are creating together.

Please look deeply and let's drain all the poison out of what I did. What more would you like to say? Will you forgive me? This will pop up every time we are scared if we don't resolve it. So when you have had a nap, or while you are waiting at the airport, let's work this through until it is done in your heart. This is an important one Adam.

Kimberley

I knew if Adam would not forgive me and if I could not forgive myself, we were doomed. Again and again we returned to this issue, that morphed into discussions on choice, trust, and feeling a "lack within ourselves" that we wanted the other to fill. Inevitably, we returned to me withholding my age. I believe that up until that moment of withholding, we had both been as honest as we knew how to be. When I consciously decided not to share my age with Adam, it was a manipulation. I sensed he would not choose to be with me because of my age, so I manipulated his decision by not giving him all of the facts. In withholding and consequently manipulating, I created a rift, a rift that grew.

Even as I write this, I continue an unveiling of the depth of my betrayal of what Adam and I were creating. My beloved mentor reminded me that the definition of betrayal is a violation of trust. Before, I did not perceive that the withholding of my age was a betrayal, because I did not want to see it. I did not, and do not, consider myself a betrayer. People who betray are ugly—and well, just wrong. If asked, I would have honestly said that I had never betrayed anyone. Holding the judgment that people who betray are ugly, made it difficult to see in myself. No, I did not speak an untruth to Adam, instead I perpetrated an untruth by what I did not say. In doing so, I violated his trust. In doing so, I betrayed him.

I did not betray him with another man, as did his ex-wife, but I betrayed him by violating our trust: a trust that to him was rare and sacred. As I write this, it has been five months since we began our adventure into love, and it is only now that I fully understand the depth of his rage at what I did. It is only now that I am taking total responsibility for my betrayal.

To many, withholding my age seems like a small thing. Something Adam should just deal with, after all, I was everything he had ever dreamt a woman could be. The fact that the age issue kept on surfacing meant if I was truly living in integrity, I had to take a more rigorous look at the impact of what I had done and why I did it. I needed to take a deeper look into the beliefs that supported my lie. If I did not, I would be cheating myself and dishonoring our relationship. I would be violating my self-trust. Why? Well, because I have committed to myself that I will dig to the bottom of any issue, regardless of the pain and discomfort that self-examination might hold.

Unwillingness to dig deep into myself and uncover my own fear, pain, manipulation and betrayal would make me a dangerous person with whom to be in a relationship. Why dangerous? Let me explain it this way: I have often taught that if your partner does not work their way to the bottom of "why" they hurt you, then they continue to be a danger to you. Saying, "I am sorry for hurting you," is not enough in a loving relationship. If the "why" someone hurt you is not resolved, then the behavior will reoccur. You are in danger of being hurt again.

If I did not stomp through the sewers of my fear and to the bottom of "why" I lied by omission, "why" I betrayed Adam in this way, I would be in serious danger of repeating the betrayal. I do not want to be a liar or a betrayer. The work it took to get to bottom of the pit of my fears was well worth the journey. Refusing the self-discovery would have cost me my integrity. Refusing to illuminate the core "why" of what I had done would make me a danger to Adam.

So I worked with my mentor and the "why" emerged. From birth I had been rejected, and love was denied. I was always too something: too small, too ugly, too sickly, too smart-mouthed, too adventurous, too independent, too, too, too… What I did with the lack of love was create a belief that I wasn't good enough to love.

This belief was so fundamentally a part of me that it created a life-long pattern of being rejected and abandoned by anyone I loved. Any man I wanted in my life was not available to love me. Deep in my Soul, beneath my conscious awareness, I was sure Adam would reject me. My belief dictated that he could not do otherwise. He would be another "almost love" that was not available. My age, the one thing I could do nothing about, would be used as an excuse to be abandoned by another unavailable man.

All of us create recurring pain in our lives, pain caused by beliefs that do not work for us. When we see the recurring patterns, we can choose to continue to live with the pain, or change the beliefs that create the reality of pain. For myself, I much preferred to change the belief and end the pain. You have to make that choice for yourself. Make the choice, and then take the action. The second half of this book, ***The Story of Change*** on page 129 shows you the four-step solution to changing your beliefs: how to end the pain of constrictive beliefs.

For Adam and me, by withholding I did not honor his right to choose for himself the age of the woman he wanted to be with. That is his right. I diminished his right. It was not up to me to decide for Adam if I was too old for him. I eventually saw that I was trying to "make him available" to me. I thought I had healed that old pattern of men not being available in the ways I wished. I was wrong. My reality made that clear. I had brought old beliefs that caused pain into this new, loving relationship.

Adam and I spoke and wrote about our feelings on this issue many times. We spoke to my mentor about it and I thought we had resolved the issue. Adam's words, his touch, his drive to plan a future with me all indicated we had survived the hurdle of my violation of trust.

CHAPTER FIVE:

13 Days, 17 Hrs, 15 Mins

LACK CAN KILL any relationship. Adam and I both entered into this relationship believing we had handled most of the "lack" in ourselves. We were wrong. I was not the only one that came into our relationship with beliefs that did not work for me. I, however, had the advantage of more years of self-examination plus two mentors, who for years had lovingly helped me grow into the woman I am. Even so, I discovered that my beliefs around my own lovability needed to be changed at an even deeper level.

Adam did not have those advantages—years of work with two mentors—and his fears began to rip into him—and into us. From the plane, en route to Kathmandu, he wrote:

SUBJECT: ***Abyss and Fear***

Hi Kimberley!

Had apoplexy on the plane…I've landed now and will spend the next 12 hours wandering around Hong Kong Airport…I'm down to 50% charge on this iPad…so, I will need to find a power adaptor…and power point…but these "fears" pale in comparison to the ones I had on the plane.

I can feel you my dear! You are present there with me as I sit in seat 65G…it is 2:30 p.m., your time and about 5:30 a.m. local, as I write this…I have been restless…but I am now wide awake and thinking about us.

What are we to each other? How can two people share a heart connection in such a short time? I know we have it, and it is a pure connection, and that sneaky bastard, my negative ego is still there with me…chipping me…I will resolve my true feelings about us, and about you, and silence that bastard once and for all!

Is it okay for a man to be so fragile? Having opened my heart to you…my (and our vulnerability)…is raw…I feel I have such a good heart and so much love to share with you, and yet doubt still surfaces. Is this because we are not holding each other's hand? We are not sharing each other's space? What does it mean to be a man sharing a heart connection with a beautiful woman and yet wrestling with these fears?

I have isolated my fears to a couple, at the moment…the main ones for me are the age difference between us, that I'm not good enough (yes, I will be working on this one), then leaving family and familiarity, my connection with my son (and "being there" for him), and being in my grandchildren and my daughter's lives in some capacity. Each of these is heavy for me to carry…and I will have to shift from where I am, to a place where I can receive your love gracefully…don't think I will be twiddling my thumbs during my time meditating, teaching, and "being" in Kathmandu.

Other questions are: where will I be, where will you be, in four months? Arghh…this is just…painful! I am in pain…my heart hurts! My thoughts are at the moment that I just don't know what to think, and I'm seeking answers in my heart...I tend to think deeply and will ruminate...probably forever!

I have adopted the philosophy of being honest with you...every step of the way...I believe I owe you, and us that...it is where I have to be...your words soothe me, but still these fears remain, is love enough? I am here, in this lifetime to love another...this is some test! I bet Higher Self is chuckling away at me...bastard!

Sorry about this email...I have reread it now a couple of times and it sounds like I'm whining to you—that is not my intention...these fears and questions are all-pervasive and I must deal with them...are you having similar fears?

Adam

How many love relationships have died on the vine because fear consumed them? How many have died because our beliefs about love—and ourselves—turn us against ourselves and, in self-defense, we threw our pain on another. How many times has one lover said to another, "It is okay sweetheart, I am here and I love you. We will be okay," and had their partner reject the truth of their love. You and I have seen this in our friends' lives, in our own lives. How many times have we thrown love away because of fear? I knew this letter was a reflection of my fear as well as Adam's. I was determined not to allow our fears to destroy us.

SUBJECT: ***Love and Strength***

My Dearest Brave Sojourner,

You are having an internal war with yourself. I will gladly obey our rule and be stable. Only one of us can be crazy at a time. You are crazed with doubt because you miss us. You have stepped outside of us and allowed your negative ego to attack you with doubt.

So I am coming to sit with you and hold your head on my breast and I will just love you. We will figure out the details. You will NEVER *abandon your children...why would you even imagine that? The sneaky bastard, your negative ego, will tear us apart if you don't pop him a good one and tell him to sit in the corner.*

Here is what I know: you are the most openly loving man who has ever graced my life. You let me tell you what is true; in fact, you demand it. You don't tell me to be less, you demand that I be more. You please me in bed (a massive understatement) and let me tell you my needs, wants, desires, and fantasies. This has never happened for me like this before. Not only do I get to tell you them, you happily and passionately give me what I desire.

You have agreed to strip away your masks, and together we see each other. I am not going to let our doubts creep in or flood in and destroy us. No, I will fight for us, simply by loving you.

You see Adam, your Achilles' heel is that you are a bundle of love. I am blessed with the "job" of loving you. We will speak the truth to each other. We will stand for each other when we fear that we are not enough, or that the other will judge us to be not enough.

I am here, right here, loving you.

Fill yourself with my scent, the feel of my skin against your body and rest your head upon my breast. I am holding you and loving you and will not let you go until you feel safe inside yourself again.

I am here with you.

Kimberley

I will write more later, but I want you to get this before you take off.

SUBJECT: **Love and Strength Part Two**

Sweetheart, I have lost track of where you might be physically in the world at this very second. However, I know where you are in spirit, and that is next to me in bed, listening to the strains of music designed to rest the brain and feed the heart. It's getting late here and the still of the night is upon me. I will drift now and see if I can get you to feel me. It is 11:18 p.m. PDT, and just past noon on Thursday in Kathmandu. Take a breath, Adam.

A new adventure. New people. Children, pretending to be older than they are…robbed, in many ways, of childhood… fill them, my love, with your gracious heart. Soon you will be busy in your new world and I will be carried in your heart. Your negative ego can make noise, but I know your courage, and you, will still it. Feel the wind on your face, Adam, I will caress you with it.

You are with me, and I am blessed that you are. Kiss me Adam, as I drift to sleep.

Think deeply my love, but feel even more.

Kimberley

SUBJECT: **Dreamland**

Ahhh dreamland…I was just there.

I love receiving your missives…they let me know you are not that far away and I can connect with you…I was writing to a girlfriend about us and was telling her that I am going to work on that negative ego, and open my heart…get back into my heart.

I asked the universe for a very special woman…one who was spiritual and full of grace, integrity, honor, and love for me…that you will fight for me…and for us…you are all of that, my sweet! I don't know how the next four months are going to pan out for us, but it is my intent that we will know each other better, understand each other's journeys, our battles and successes, from now until we decide not to…I want to know your desires and interests, what makes you "crinkly" with anger, joyous, sad, and frightened…I want to know your favorite everything (yes, even vegetable)…I'm guessing potato (yam), I want to know your favorite chocolate…I want to know why you struggle, like me, to receive the love of someone else.

As I do my internal work, I will tell you of my findings and seek your guidance as to interpretation…I want to know everything about you…if you will share, you will find a grateful man, loved beyond measure by a gorgeous and extraordinary woman…I am genuine and loving…you may not find in me the comfort that other men who are used to wealth may find in their surroundings, but I am rich in other ways and I have it to give to you…if you will accept…we will be rich in love and spirit…your happiness, and knowledge that you are loved is my priority…I don't know how much someone with my ambition to work with troubled youth (or just youth without a role model) makes, but I'm guessing it's not that much…I am thinking already of someone I can approach, to write work references for me…I had some ideas.

I trust you are sleeping well and resting in my peace…a beautiful woman.

Adam xoxoxo

And yes, never stop drawing me to you!

SUBJECT: **Re: To Dreamland I Go**

My Darling,

I woke very early and heard you call. I read your love missive to me, and then laid back down with my heart filled. I want to share every part of myself with you, even when it is the not so pretty, and sometimes downright ugly.

My darn phone is down (long story), but I cannot text you today. I will try and write later. I'm not sure how I will be feeling, and whether I will need solitude while my mentor and I are working.

I do know that your missive made my heart sing, and that I am with you as I feel you with me.

Be patient with me this weekend, my love, while I work intensively with my mentor. You will be deep in my heart. Holding you close to my heart and whispering in your ear, "Thank you for the beautiful love missive."

LDK (Long Deep Kiss)

K

Adam and I survived his first wave of all-consuming fear, and we once again settled in to plan our future together. We hardly had time to catch our breaths, when I was scheduled to begin a two-day, full-immersion private intensive with one of my trusted mentors. I knew down to my bones that I would be different on the other side of this intensive. My intention was clear from the beginning: I would go into the intensive with one goal, that I would emerge "more." I trusted that my mentor and I would create the precise path for me to travel. I knew I needed to share every step that I could with Adam, so he could choose to journey with me.

Journeying the path of growing together would be key for Adam and me. If one grew and the other did not, that would create a void between us. We knew that and had spoken about that risk to our relationship. It was a risk we had to take. Neither one of us would ever be content with a life without the adventure of growth. Knowing all of this, and with Adam's total support, I began another adventure into myself.

CHAPTER SIX:

15 Days, 8 Hrs, 4 Mins

AS ADAM AND I had discussed my impeding intensive, I think on some level he was every bit as excited as me. His encouragement eased my fear that we would grow apart. No matter what my expectations were, I could not envision just how different I would be at the end of what was about to unfold.

Day one was intense beyond description. So much of it will never be told by mere words. I sat in silence a long time after we were done for the day. I had so much to share, yet I needed space and solitude.

Silently, the sea and I sat together. I did not think. I just sat and allowed myself to be. Time moved without my awareness. When I emerged from my metamorphic chrysalis, the sun was setting and I was ready to share with my beloved.

SUBJECT: ***Paradigm Shift***

It has been a paradigm-shifting day and I want to share with you. I am only half-done with the intensive, but I will share what I know about myself, love, intimacy, and my relationships with men.

Today we worked on vulnerability, intimacy and humility. I promised you the facts of what happened so you could always make a choice. Give me a little while to get some food and I will write to you.

Have a great day my love.

K

SUBJECT: **Re: Paradigm Shift**

I love paradigm-shifting days! I get excited by the prospect of something new…new opportunities and perspectives… get some food, gorgeous, and sit while you think, feel and digest…I have just had a coffee and a breakfast…they just put an incense stick near me…they are so thoughtful :-) I love incense.

I am getting settled here…in my spirit and in my body…I am going to design a routine to work on all I am…mind, body and spirit! Super excited about it too: yoga, meditation and nutrition, plus teaching and new experiences.

Thank you for the work you are doing (and for sharing it with me)…I know you are doing it for you…but I am here, learning and being with you as you confront these issues…and I also have a vested interest…in that I will benefit from your shifting paradigm…lucky me :-) whichever way it goes…you will be more! I'm so excited for you…for us…and what we choose to create…take your time and integrate what there is for you…I am patient and will wait for you…

If I were with you I would have my arms around you, massaging your shoulders and gently kissing your neck…feeling your warmth, your feminine spirit and your love…such a joyous place to be …

I had a fantasy about us making love last night! My imagination runs wild with us…Mmmmmm.

Write when you can…but don't make it a priority until you feel it is right to do so…I will be here.

A xoxoxoxo

SUBJECT: ***I Have Tried to Put into Words***

Hello Love,

Your love missive filled me with smiles, dancing joy, and warm soothing love. Thank you!

I so appreciate your patience and your willingness to let me do this in my own time. Rather than writing in my journal, I'm going to talk to you about what happened today, as much to help me integrate it as to invite you on the journey. So it probably will not be organized or in any definitive order. But I trust that you will feel the essence and the bravery that it takes to share this with you.

Let me start by saying that I entered this intensive with my mentor, totally open to any topics that he wanted to deal with. After working with him for well over five years, I trust that he knows the topics that need to be addressed more than I. That is not to give my power away, no, it's rather about trusting his insights.

He began by saying we were going to celebrate how far I have come. And then he said we would be working on vulnerability, intimacy, and humility. These are things I have been working on now for several years with focused intensity.

As you know, because we discussed it, arrogance, superiority and control are/were defense mechanisms that I used to survive.

The day continued with me feeling my vulnerability which, if I was pressed to describe it, I would have to say it felt like a circle of warmth and peace about the size of a grapefruit between my 2nd and 3rd chakras.

You might well ask what does vulnerability feel like. I think it probably feels differently for each and every one of us. What I'm discovering is that vulnerability is not just one thing; it is multi-faceted. I learned today that vulnerability and intimacy are the doorways through which the type of life I want to live flows.

In short, I cannot have the life I want without being vulnerable and intimate.

I will digress for just a second and share that we were talking function not form. This means that I truly do not care what the form of my life looks like as long as the functions are in place. Form follows function…in physics and architecture…and life. So when I program, or create in my life, I am striving for my functions: joy, adventure, mattering, positive impact, abundance, happiness…if I have these then the form doesn't matter. I will be fulfilled.

So, back to my adventure…vulnerability and intimacy are key-and-lock. Vulnerability means being simultaneously aware of both my weaknesses and my strengths, and so much more. Intimacy means closeness, openness, tenderness, vulnerability, knowing and being known, caring, and loving. As we talked about vulnerability and intimacy, my mentor asked me to speak of our relationship in regards to those. We spoke about your integrity and the purity of it. We spoke about the loving man that you are. We spoke about your fears of not being enough. And we spoke about the bravery of your "walkabout." We spoke of your age prejudice and my prejudice around money.

Then we began to explore resonance and essence. In short, we looked at what paradigm created the men I have had in my life in the past. Men who on one level or another were unavailable to me: emotionally, economically, spiritually, maturity-wise, etc. Men, who in one way or another, did not fulfill my needs.

And that last sentence is THE paradigm shift. It is not a man's responsibility to fill my needs. It is not a man's responsibility to fulfill any "lack" in me. Dear Adam, I can say the words, but knowing that on an intellectual level is so different to rewiring yourself to accommodate a new paradigm. We did that rewiring today.

Our potential problem, yours and mine, is that I was standing in the old paradigm when we met. I was looking for a man to fill me when we began. Oh, on a much more discreet and perhaps subtle level than needy women appear to have, but fill my needs nevertheless.

I have thought for quite a while that men were preferences in my life. What I discovered today, on a deeply profound level, was that was not true. I wanted one to fill my lack; to love me so I didn't have to truly love myself; to love me so I felt loveable; to love me so I could feel good about myself. While I have worked at these "lacks" for years, now there they were again on a whole new level. On a smaller level, perhaps, but still there, I also created relationships with men who wanted me to fill their "lack." How could that not be true? Of course that is the resonance match I would pull in. No matter how "good" it looked, what was true was that there was always one part of the man that didn't fit for me. Why? Because then I could maintain superiority. I could maintain some level of control. I could be safe. Aha! again a "lack." I wanted the man to "fill me" by being "less than," so I could maintain control, and the illusion of safety.

I have worked diligently on these, yet today, or maybe because I have worked diligently on them, we shifted the paradigm. Dearest Adam, I can't tell you exactly how it happened because it was a combination of things. But this is what I understand now: if there is any "lack" in me that I want you to fill, if there is any "lack" in you that you want me to fill, then we are in a paradigm of fear. From that paradigm there is no level of freedom that would satisfy either one of us for very long.

Filling what is lacking in us for ourselves is key to having a relationship based on preference. For instance, you free me in bed. You listen to what my preferences are and you do not turn away. You give me permission, by your behavior and your acceptance, to be sensuous, alive and passionate. The man that you are feeds the woman in me. This is, by our societal standards, totally healthy and wonderful. But it is not healthier or wonderful. I need to come to our bed feeling whole and sensuous and sexy. The fact that you also feel that is a plus, but not a necessity, for me feeling those things about myself.

If you come to the relationship feeling not enough, looking for proof from me that you are enough, or wanting me to fill that hole, then we are in the old paradigm again.

You could reasonably ask what's wrong with the old paradigm. The problem with the old paradigm is that it is based on fear and need, which we cover up rather than face. We dress up our relationships so they look pretty. Underneath a cauldron is boiling, because fear and need will eventually find their way to the surface. Then we blame the other for not fixing the fear or fulfilling the need. Oh, but let's not stop there, no, it is even more insidious than that. The truth is, I realize now that I have wanted to keep the old paradigm in place because it was safer. It was safer for reasons that might surprise you.

I think most of us do not want to get to this new paradigm because it means we must stay conscious in our relationship at all times. It means that a relationship is a constant and continuous choice. There are no guarantees. There is no happy-ever-

after without the consciousness. There is no promise or commitment that guarantees the future. And that is why we hold onto the old paradigm. Even if that paradigm is virtually guaranteed to undermine our relationships in some fashion.

In the new paradigm, we come to a relationship, if indeed we want a relationship, with our needs filled. We have done the work to fill our "lack." We do not expect the other to be responsible for that filling.

No matter how "lack" might be disguised in the socially acceptable premise of what a man gives a woman and what a woman gives a man, it is still "lack."

In the new paradigm I am different, I have become new. The new me has a resonance or beingness in the world different from the woman I was just two days before. This new me, this new resonance, which emanated from me is more authentically vulnerable. I replaced "lack" with vulnerability. This new paradigm is filled with intimacy, not control. It is filled with humility, which means at any moment on any day, the relationship could be over or elevated into something new. Not because something went wrong, but because we chose again. We strive for a promise of happy-ever-after so that we do not have to stay conscious and diligent. We want a guarantee, and the written piece of paper that proves that this person is going to be committed to us forever. The new paradigm is filled with freedom. Freedom to choose, at any given moment, whether we love each other or not.

After rereading this I realize I have failed to communicate the true essence of the new paradigm, because these words sound like "sure, I knew that." In the new paradigm I am so connected with myself, with the flow of dreams and imaginings, based in vulnerability, intimacy and humility that I resonate differently.

I am different in a fundamental way. I am so sorry Adam, I cannot find the words.

I discovered today, and I hasten to say that this is all very new, that vulnerability must be part of my core essence. I have discovered that it is nothing like I thought it was. Vulnerability is joy and power and curiosity, and more. As I said, I am just discovering what it really is.

And here is the hook, I must stay conscious all the time, and choose our relationship from moment to moment. So, because I created you, remember I believe I create my own reality—all of it—from the old paradigm, I must give up the relationship that is based on that old paradigm.

If we are going to create a future it must be from the paradigm of not bringing "lack" into the relationship. The thought of losing you, even based on the old paradigm, was very painful to me. It filled me with fear. I mourned it. And yet I'm willing to give it all up so I can live this life that is based in choice. To live a life where I am vulnerable and intimate with myself. A life where the vulnerability and the intimacy that radiates from me attracts people who are filled with them as well.

I have created men and women in my life filled with "lack," once again so I could stay safe by being superior. It looked very good. Oh, what a good person I was that I gave to person A or B or C. But it was all to stay safe. It was all about staying in control. And my control is insidious and sneaky. I must be more and more conscious of it. Even the choice of explaining all of this to you, even after I promised you that I would, was a struggle. Before I caught myself, I told myself that you do not have the foundation I have, so how could you understand all of this? What arrogance on my part. What superiority. What crap.

K

At this point I took a break from my missive and sat with the ocean. I listened to the waves and let them anchor my resolve. I let the wind blow through my hair and whisper words of celebration to me. I looked across the ocean and wondered. I knew that Adam was brilliant. You have not had an opportunity to sit and speak with him, but he is nothing short of brilliant. He has a mind that can hold multiple levels of information simultaneously. His mind would take all of this in, but would his heart? I knew that his constricting beliefs were still in place and they would taint his perception of what I was saying. I wondered how he would interpret my words. Would he think I did not want to be in a relationship with him? Or, as I hoped, could he hear that I wanted to begin anew? I wanted to begin again from my newly found paradigm based in tenderness, humility, vulnerability, intimacy and wholeness. I did not know what Adam would choose, but I knew I had to finish trying to explain who I had become.

CHAPTER SEVEN:

15 Days, 10 Hrs, 0 Mins

I SAT DOWN with the fresh smell of the sea and the soft breeze, and continued.

SUBJECT: ***I Have Tried to Put into Words...(MORE)***

Adam,

As you have so valiantly pointed out, it is never my place to decide for you. I can only offer you all the information and allow you to choose the same, just as you allow me to choose.

My mentor asked me—after this work—which took hours, "What do you feel about your relationship now?" And Adam, what I felt was hope. As I treat you with respect, as I offer you the information as cleanly and clearly as I can, I have hope. I know, in ways that I cannot explain, that while you are away in these four months, opportunities will come to you that you have not dreamt of before. And it very well might take you down the road that does not include our relationship. I knew this when I saw you off at the airport. I knew as I saw you standing in that door, that I might never see you again.

From this new paradigm, where I am seated in vulnerability, intimacy, and humility I know it as well. But my love, I want you to have that freedom. I want you to be freed to choose what fits for you. I love you. Because I do I want you to be on your Soul's path. I want you to have the most abundantly juicy life you can have. On a daily basis, I want you to be surrounded in your own self-love because you are following your Soul's path and feeding yourself with your choices. I want these things for you. And I want these things for myself. I hope we walk the path together but I love me and I love you enough to want what is right and true for each of us.

I don't know if I have done an adequate job of explaining the ineffable. Perhaps if you close your eyes and meld with me you will find the truth there, more than exists in these inadequate words.

A long time ago, I read a romance novel where the couple got married in a Gypsy ceremony. And I have always remembered it; perhaps it was a herald of these lessons that I am learning. In the ceremony, the words bounding the lovers went something like this, "I love you. And I love you so much that should this love ever dwindle I commit to you that I will turn you loose so that someone else can love you as much as I love you today."

This, of course, could for some be a total cop-out. It could be a true lack of commitment, intent, and intimacy. Not so for me. It is in my mind and heart a true vow of humility. When I live in humility, I allow every person to be new from moment to moment. Humility allows me to be new from moment to moment. Humility allows the world to be new. Without humility how can anything ever change? Humility is incredibly powerful. It demands incredible integrity. It is pure, and whole, and true.

My learning is not done. I am integrating and my Higher Self will come while I sleep, and help me even more. And there is an entire day tomorrow. I certainly don't know who I will be tomorrow night. I don't know who I am tonight. I am more. I am certainly more whole. And Adam, from this new paradigm, I love you. And I am going to enjoy loving you. From this new paradigm of vulnerability, I hope you will choose to explore with me.

Smiling right into your eyes,

Kimberley

I cannot even imagine how getting a missive like this, years ago, would have affected me. How would I have felt reading these words before I had begun my uphill journey of growth? Poorly, I think. But I had promised. I committed before I began the intensive that I would withhold nothing. I honored that promise to the best of my ability.

From my new paradigm I was willing for Adam to say goodbye. I would mourn, but I was willing. I would not be torn to pieces because I loved myself in an entirely different way. As I lay down to sleep that night, I hoped and I was at peace. As I slept, two missives found their way to me.

SUBJECT: ***My Head Hurts!***

Hi Gorgeous…:-)

I have written some thoughts in response to your first day with your mentor…but my head is now hurting and I wanted to sleep on them before I sent them to you…as I want to make sure the thoughts I send to you are cogent…at the moment…because there is so much there, I feel my email is a bit "everywhere," so I will go through it again before I send it to you…but the highlights are:

I'm in awe of your work!

I love your honesty and sharing…I have realized that I too have a lack...and that is to be loved by you...but I feel this is a human condition rather than a lack...I think we all want the love of another human...it's that what makes us have relationships...I come to this relationship wanting to be loved by you...I am perfect and deserve a woman like you...I honor your commitment to shift paradigms and do not fear losing you should this be an outcome...whilst I would be sad, I like your romance-story commitment to love. That there be no greater love than to let someone go to be loved by another capable of giving more...(Wow...I like that)...that's what I call true love...that's what I have so far...but I'm sure there is more.

You have had a huge day...we are both changing.

God bless Gorgeous :-)

Adam xoxoxoxo

SUBJECT: ***Re: I Have Tried to Put into Words***

Hello Gorgeous,

"We must cultivate our garden" (Voltaire 1759).

See...I told you I like paradigm shifts! Thank you for sharing your session outcomes with me. I know they are deeply personal and offer insights into you, both as a person and a growing Soul. I believe we are like the gardens envisioned by Voltaire; the day we do not lovingly tend them, cultivate them and live in their beauty, is the day we turn away from this life's purpose. I, for one, love this quote...may we both always tend and cultivate our gardens, do the work that is required of us to become more than we are.

To create a relationship of abundance, not one (and I agree with you) where we look to another to fill a need. I have been in relationships where I have rescued another...my 21-year marriage was one of those…my ex attracted me to her life to fill a need for security and safety; I attracted her because I needed to rescue her from uncertainty and give her that safety and security…and to be the person she wanted me to be. This was far from my authentic self and the relationship was swathed in fear…and doomed to fail. I don't want a relationship like that.

I have now created a woman who has those attributes I mentioned in my last missive, not because I lacked any of them, but because I could connect at an emotional and spiritual level. The fact that we can also connect on the physical is fantastic…(though, as you know, I have a prejudice here that I am working on).

You wrote:

"I have thought for quite a while that men were a preference in my life. What I discovered today on the deeply profound level was that was not true. I wanted one to fill my "lack." Love me so I don't have to truly love myself. Love me so I feel love. Love me and let me love you so I can feel good about myself."

This is exactly true for myself…except in reverse.

So what you are saying is that successful relationships are based on not seeking a "lack" in another for some form of self-fulfillment, because this is a form of negativity? Ipso facto, if a relationship is based on filling a lack in one's self, then that relationship…ours…is heading towards a relationship based in fear…i.e., a doomed relationship? This is my reading too.

So, to my feeling of not being enough for you…I am a perfect being in exactly the right place and time for my learning. However, just writing this email to you has highlighted to me that I do indeed look to you (and our relationship) to fill a hole in my life…my need to be loved, is directly related to being a priority in your life, your love fills a hole in my view of myself…

I believe as a human, I crave to be loved…and to love. This is what I was put here to learn…and that is my "lack" I will look to you to fill…I would love to see your mentor's take on this.

If this was to be considered a "lack," I realize there are two aspects to it…one: that I love myself and don't care that you love me or not…or two: that I love myself and care that you love me…I prefer the second one…the first represents to me a loveless relationship…so there is a hole I need to be filled by your love in our relationship…is the craving to be loved, touched, vulnerable, and intimate with another person a "lack"?

Perhaps you attracted me from your old paradigm of needing to be superior to my inferior earning potential? Which feeds directly into your insecurity (fear) about me being able to support you, and us should it come to that. I cannot change this fear and, as you say, it is not my responsibility to do so…just as it is not your responsibility to address my fears.

That said, I am in awe of your intent to shift your paradigm to remove it from your psyche and make yourself vulnerable to it…and then to tell me you are still able to love me in spite of the shift, has stunned me to my core. You truly are a magnificent, courageous, and very brave woman!

So, what of me? A blunt assessment: I know I come into a relationship with you with a couple of "lacks." And the premise is that you will fill those lacks through your love for me…and I too can feel good about myself…my "lack" is also believing I'm good enough, and not having money to live.

I realize also, that these lacks are severely hindering my vulnerability to you and therefore destroying my chance to be truly intimate with you, and with myself. Pardon the French…but… well…F&%! I feel that I must work on deservability and resolve it before I can be intimate on any level…haha…the* *thought just crossed my mind, that I could ask you to help me in this regard…then I realized that this is exactly the point…I have a "lack" and I'm looking to you to help me fill it, to fill it for me …again…F*&%!*

I don't know what to feel…I understand your paradigm shift, and given my "lacks," have reservations that I am the man for you, that I deserve such an extraordinary woman…or in fact the man for any woman (that sounds ugly…and disrespectful to women…but that's not my intent)…not seeking sympathy here…just voicing my negative ego thoughts out loud…as I have never met a person who does not have a "lack" in some regard…have you? I would love to meet them…perhaps the Dalai Lama?

I need to think some more about this…as I'm sure you'll understand that there is a lot to integrate.

Thank you for your caring for me…and the sharing. I did not feel your arrogance and don't beat yourself up for sharing it. Remember you are perfect!

Adam xoxoxo

SUBJECT: ***I Do Love You So***

Hello Sweetheart,

First and forever foremost, thank you. You have once again impressed me with your willingness to process with me and to stand for yourself and for us. I guess I'm going to start by telling you what happened today and then I'll write a second missive responding to the one that you just sent me. I am more seated in vulnerability, intimacy, and humility. Yet they are fragile, they are new. I am requiring of myself that this becomes the new foundation of who I am. I must, because they are the doorways, the keys to the life I want to live, and also because the planet is in dire need of these things. Standing in this resonance, in fact becoming this resonance, is now a primary focus of my life. I understand in a way that is beyond words that this must become prime. The prime directive, if you will.

There is a piece, a critical piece of my learning, that I forgot to tell you yesterday…there was so much to share…it is no wonder that I forgot. But it is the glue that holds it all together, or perhaps better said, the TNT that would blow it apart—and that is: agendas. Agenda means having an ulterior motive. Walk with me down this path for a moment, sweetheart…I have agendas for almost everything I do. When with a client, I want them to get better. This, in the face of it, seems like a wonderful thing to desire. However, if I examine why I want them to be better, it is because I want to feel good about myself. My mentor once told me that this was greed. He told me I was greedy. I didn't understand that because I considered myself to be a generous person. As he explained it, it made more sense. I want my clients to get better for me. Not just for them. What was more true was that I wanted them to be better so I could feel good about myself. I wanted them to get better and tell other people, so other people will admire me. I wanted the applause. See how important I am, how good am I at what I do? Don't you appreciate and respect me even more now? This is greed and I have worked diligently on ending it.

Follow me further through this labyrinth, my love. So if I pick apart absolutely everything I want, every dream, every goal, every desire; they all appear in the consensus as being altruistic, or at the very least positive goals. But I must examine each for agendas. One might reasonably ask what is wrong with agendas if the ulterior motive does good in the world?

Here is a problem with agendas…they leave no room for the

magic of the moment. The universe, God, Goddess, All That Is, cannot work their magic when we have agendas. Think about that. Really think about that. Maybe take a walk, and ponder the things that are important to you in your life and search underneath for agendas. Reach in deeply, search for ulterior motives that are not healthy.

There is nothing wrong with wanting things for ourselves. It is not about wanting something; it is about the "why" of wanting it. When we want to function on the level where vulnerability, intimacy, and humility are the doorways to a life beyond reckoning, we must give up agendas or the ulterior motive for what we desire.

We can want anything just because it brings us joy or happiness. Then there is no agenda or ulterior motive.

The problem usually is that our agendas and "lack" pair up. I want you to love me so I will be kind, thoughtful, giving, etc. If I care about you in these ways because it gives me joy to do so, then there is no lack or agenda. If I care for you this way so you will love me and fill the hole in me, then there is a mating of "lack" and agenda.

So let's look at my agenda of loving you. I addressed this a bit last night and you addressed it by saying, "...my need to be loved, is directly related to being a priority in your life, your love fills a hole in my view of myself...I believe as a human, I crave to be loved...and to love. This is what I was put here to learn...and that is my 'lack', I will look to you to fill..."

Adam, if you had asked me before I entered this intensive if there was anything "wrong" with these type of agendas I would have said "of course not." But I understand more now. Let me try to explain in words what I learned, in essence.

A quick aside, it is extraordinary that you picked up as much as you did from my single missive to you…you are indeed an extraordinary man. I want you to know, my dear love, that no matter what happens to us I believe this.

So what did I learn in essence? It is this, that love cannot have an agenda. We cannot love to get love. We cannot love to prove our worth or to get someone else to prove it by loving us. We cannot love to fill holes in ourselves.

You said you were put on this earth to love. You came to learn all aspects of love, as did I. We reflect back and forth to each other the shining light that is love. We also reflect back and forth to each other agendas that poison love.

As I described in my last missive, I wanted you to love me so I could feel loveable, so I could bask in the love you send because I needed it to fill me. I was not whole, so I had an agenda that if I loved you, you would love me back and that would fill my "lack." See that damn pairing, agenda, and "lack"?

So now let's take it deeper into the chasm of the labyrinth. True love and agendas cannot exist simultaneously, if we are to really understand the depth of love. You ask if the Dalai Lama is the only one who loves not to fill "lack"…the answer is no…but there is not enough of us. If we, those who knowingly carry pieces of the God, Goddess, All That Is, light within us, pollute that love then we have not done what we came to do.

We must learn to love without agenda. If we believe in Eastern philosophy we would deny ourselves; that would end all agendas, wouldn't it? We would reject our needs and wants. This is not what I am saying. Rather I am saying that we meet our own needs. I must be so filled with self-love that there is no "lack" of love in me.

So when my child-self cries out, "Somebody love me and make me feel safe," I must go to her (inside myself) and love her, and provide for her safety. When my adolescent cries out and says, "Make me feel beautiful, make me know that I can grow into a woman," then I must help her feel beautiful, and show her how to become a woman. When my negative ego says, "This is all a bunch of crap, don't listen…if you do, you will be alone. You will be without love," I must silence him.

Again, my negative ego challenges, "If you do not have a hole to fill then you will not need, and if you do not need then no one will love you at all. How will you survive without love?" I must still my negative ego and reply, "I will take care of it."

If any of the aspects of me cry out for love, then I must hear their call and respond. When I do, I am more able to fill myself with love. When I recognize these needs in me, and fill them, that is a way of loving myself. When I stand in the essence of vulnerability, intimacy, and humility, that is a way of loving myself. When I respect myself and others by setting boundaries that honor my vulnerability, intimacy, and humility then I am loving myself.

How, Adam, could you possibly do any of these things for me? You could not. More dangerously, you would try and fail and you would forever more feel "not enough." Feeling "not enough" comes from standards that are impossible to meet. If I, as a woman, required these things from you, even in the secret parts of my heart, then I am in the process of helping to destroy you.

Just as importantly, I separate myself from true love, the deep love that can only be experienced when I am anchored in self-love. The love so many seek, the pure love without agendas, can only be achieved if you love yourself first.

In turn, my true self-love can only be experienced when I am seated in vulnerability, intimacy and humility. That love, the one rooted in self-love, which I am just beginning to taste, is the love that I believe all of humankind has been searching for.

It is love without struggle. It is love without agendas. It is love without the price we have thought we had to pay. The price of this love is letting go of our "lack" by fulfilling our needs ourselves. The price of this love is learning to love ourselves. The price of this love is forgiving ourselves when we mess up, as we will. The price of this love is nothing like we believed it would be.

I love you. It is a joy to love you. I have learned and I am "more." So I refuse to poison my love for you by filling it with agendas or "lack." So, if I love myself so completely that I do not "lack," will I receive the love you give to me so beautifully? The answer is yes. I want your love, without agendas or ulterior motives, for the sheer joy of it. If I love you for the sheer beauty of you, and have no agendas, will that love hold brave and true? The answer is yes.

K

I stilled my hand as I wrote this last "yes." Loving Adam had come easily and I wanted to love him. I know part of "why," is because he is so loveable. I wish he had known how loveable he was, but I digress. I sat for the longest time just loving Adam. Loving him for the sheer joy of it. So I sat with my love for Adam and allowed it to fill me.

CHAPTER EIGHT:

16 Days, 8 Hrs, 40 Mins

I DO NOT know how long I sat in love, but when I surfaced I was ready to continue my missive of love and understanding.

SUBJECT: ***I Do Love You So…(More)***

So Adam, keeping true to the metaphor, let us head into the heart of the labyrinth…doing anything in our life that includes agendas, keeps magic from happening. It keeps miracles from happening. God, Goddess, All That Is cannot participate in our lives in the way that they wish, if we do not leave room for magic and miracles. So we beseech God, and yet leave no room for God to answer in a way that God wishes.

God, Goddess, All That Is, has gifted us with choice. The Goddess always says, "Yes." Do you want a miserable life? She will weep for your request, but she will say, "Yes." Do you want a life filled with dreams beyond your reckoning? The answer is, "Yes." No matter what we choose in this playground we created for learning, God, Goddess, All That Is will never take choice away from us. It was a gift; they will not take it back.

If I live in "lack" and do not fulfill it myself, but rather expect you to fill me, I make you a prisoner. You have told me that you were in a kind of prison in your marriage. I will not participate in making you a prisoner by asking you to do what you could not possibly do. The gift of freedom, the gift of choice, was bestowed on all of humankind by God, Goddess, All That Is. For my part, I trust that their love and magic is bigger than mine. I trust that their dreams for me are beyond what I would dream for myself. If holding onto my agendas keeps God, Goddess, All That Is from working their love and magic in my life, then I say, give up the damn agendas. In short, agendas rule out the magic of the moment.

Agendas kill the true brilliance of love. I will practice being without agendas, sometimes fall flat on my face…forgiving myself and trying again. But I will fill my own "lack" and love myself to the brim and over. I will discover, and end my agendas. I will love because it brings me joy. As I've said before, one might ask if loving for the joy of it is an agenda. I say no, because joy is not about wanting something from the other. It is not about building self-esteem or worth based on who or what we love. It is not about what we want our love to say about us…what we want our love to prove is true about us.

So, in the heart of the labyrinth, my love, I stand waiting for you, not out of expectation that you must jump through any hoops or even agree to a word I have written. But rather, to say, I love you regardless of what you do.

That is the best description I can give, sweetheart. I will comment on what you've written in your last email, but for now I only have one more thought.

My last thought is that we are indeed not perfect, nor do we want to be. We want to go home to God, Goddess, All That Is.

In order to do that we must grow and change, not because the Goddess requires it of us, but because we want to find out what it feels like to grow and change. How empty would any level of existence be if there was not always room to grow and be more?

People have taught us that we are perfect just the way we are, and that situations are perfect just the way they are. This simply is not true. I am not perfect, nor do I strive to be. What I am, is deserving of love for no reason at all. By virtue of my birth, I'm deserving of all the goodness, truth, beauty, and love that the universe has to offer. This is what people mean when they say we are perfect. I am not perfect. I am deserving.

What I also am is forgivable. I am forgivable. I will make mistakes, it is expected that I will. What I am is beautiful. What I am is learning to be more and more loving. I think I understand what you meant by using the word "perfect," and the comfort that was intended. But I ask you to entertain the thought in a different way. Our subconscious minds have no sense of humor. They are absolutely concrete. If you say you are perfect then it has no reason to help you, no reason to throw its significant weight behind your endeavors. Because, after all, you are already perfect so why help you grow? Do you see? The subconscious listens to all that we say, all that we do. The computer, if you will accept the metaphor, is always recording our orders. Besides, my dearest love, our vulnerability, our lack of perfection is what we truly love in each other.

I love your willingness to walk this labyrinth with me. It impresses me; your courage impresses me…beyond measure. I will write more, maybe tonight or tomorrow.

It has indeed been a life-changing weekend. I do love you.

K

SUBJECT: **Re: Overwhelmed**

Dearest Love,

I realize that sharing and downloading with you can be very overwhelming. I was there and I am overwhelmed.

I woke up this morning, 12 hours after my intensive, in emotional pain. I know all pain is based in a separation from love. I also know it is my responsibility to love myself, and I do, and will be better at it. With that said, I miss your touch. I know I must move forward and I know you must choose for yourself. I am holding that we can do this together…I get really fearful…then I get settled…in short, I am a mess.

After working so intensively, I need time just to be and to think. I do wish I could sleep in your arms. See, thoughts all over the place. I am a mess…but in a good way.

I spoke with a friend early this morning, one who is walking a similar path. It was a relief to speak with someone who is going thru a similar process of filling his own "lack" and ending agendas. He gave me comfort by saying that ending agendas is a process, and that I must stay diligent and filled with integrity. I knew this, but hearing him share his journey reminded me I did not have to do it perfectly, just with conscious integrity.

I told him about you and this is what he said (and I paraphrase), "How wonderful that Adam is a man totally committed to loving, and understanding love. Doing all of this from a place of integrity. An integrity that matches and can supersede your own."

That was such a comforting thing to hear from someone whom I respect, and who has no agenda. He was just sharing his observations. For me, it was a reminder of what you have repeatedly shared with me; you came into this lifetime to understand love, and be loving. I am so grateful for that. I am so very grateful for you regardless of where we journey. My heart swells full of gratitude for you!

K

SUBJECT: ***A Testing Path...For Both of Us***

Dearest Kimberley,

Thank you for your missives and sharing your learning and also your concerns regarding being overwhelmed. I can tell you that I too am overwhelmed, and have retreated to my internal "man-cave" to ponder and ruminate over my shame, deservability, fears, lacks, agendas, getting to my truth, and again asking the question of myself...what is "true love"? Just when I think I have an idea, that elusive vixen jumps into the bushes, and I again appear clueless (but ever closer)...Dah!

I would ask you to be patient with me as I analyze and dissect my thoughts and beliefs. I am not conscious of my agendas...but I know they are there...I am not fully aware of my "lack"...and again, I know they are there. I have deservability issues that I intend to meditate on and pry from my conscious and subconscious minds. I know I have fears, about you, and about our relationship, which I have mostly not dealt with...but will...and I know they are a block to what we can create...I know that your love alone is powerless to save this relationship...it is a joint endeavor and both of us must approach with love and care...I do know that I am not ready to commit my soul and my love (be truly intimate) to anyone until I have addressed these issues...(and more probably as I tease them out)...I know also that there are many obstacles to my pure self-love. But my dearest Kimberley, this is exactly why I am here! To explore the depths of love, my frailties as a human, and their impact on the love I can have for another...and then to resolve each one, so that the love I offer is not sullied with fear, lack, agenda, deservability or shame.

Please do not underestimate my resolve to understand my journey in this lifetime, and do not worry for me. My path to vulnerability, intimacy, and true understanding of my Self, with no agendas, is a long but very worthy road to travel.

I am, and will be, eternally grateful to you for showing me...in the fullness of your love for me and with strength and caring...a path to bliss...a transcendent relationship (my fantasy)...how can I not be in awe of your beauty, caring and love? I am truly blessed that you have chosen to show it to me and I am humble and soooo grateful as the trailhead stands before me, that I have metaphorically fallen to my knees weeping.

I sense that you feel me slipping from you, and us, as you show me a path to my fantasy...I will hold the space for you...and for us. I know you to be courageous and brave...as from a place of integrity you speak to my higher good, at potential cost to yourself...I see in you, that woman making those vows at the "Gypsy" wedding...I am so glad you are in my life.

As I journey and start my hike, it must be alone...I will absolutely share with you what I see as I ascend, the wild animals I will meet along the way, and the knowing I re-discover... I am excited to start!

Adam xoxoxoxo

As I read Adam's missive to me I smiled with sadness. I had felt him stepping back from me and our relationship, since I was hit with the premonition at the airport. Yet, his emails had remained full of love and it gave me hope. From this new paradigm, the one where I am seated in vulnerability, humility, tenderness, and intimacy, I could feel between the lines, and behind his words. After sixteen days, countless missives of love, and a few precious days of being together, I could feel him stepping back.

Adam wrote, "I do know that I am not ready to commit my soul and my love (be truly intimate) to anyone until I have addressed these issues…" His perception was true, but still it saddened me, while at the same time I celebrated his clarity.

Adam's intuitiveness, the part of him that held him in good stead in the world of high stakes security, was evident when he wrote, "I sense that you feel me slipping from you, and us, as you show me a path to my fantasy…I will hold the space for you…and for us. I know you to be courageous and brave…"

The words had not been spoken, yet he knew that I felt the loss of his total commitment to us. You might not see or feel it, not yet, for his love missives were filled with words of hope and commitment. But for me, I knew he was stepping back. What I did not know was if it was permanent—was he saying good-bye? Or did he need time to find himself.

SUBJECT: ***A Testing Path…For Both of Us***

Hello Love,

Our emails crossed in cyberspace. I am confused. You say you need to walk this journey alone. I understand, I think? Did you want me to back off? I do feel you slip away…but I know it is to find and recreate yourself. What I do not know is what kind of communication you want. In the last few days I have written to you a lot…yes, a whole lot…I wanted to share and in doing so give myself something to read again and again to re-evaluate where I am in any given moment, based on what I thought and felt during, and coming out of, the intensive.

I know when I go inside I need to be alone. I need the solitude until I don't. So Adam you have to tell me what you want, or I will just keep pleasing myself and writing to you when I want to feel you.

Sweet kiss to you love,

K

SUBJECT: **Re: A Testing Path...For Both of Us**

Sorry my dearest...email and the written word are so easy to misinterpret...:-)

No, I don't want you to back off! I want you to keep writing... and share my journey of discovery with me...I want to share your discovery with you.

I'm not slipping away...but becoming more introspective as I journey into my own heart...

It's true...our relationship is not one like I've ever had before... and I don't know what it means...or whether I will ever make love with you again, but I do know that we are sharing our personal growth and I feel there is a strong and growing bond between us ...

I ask for your patience...I am catching up to where you are, but this will take time...I don't need anything from you, but I am grateful to you for sharing ...

Adam xoxoxoxo

I continued to write to Adam, and he shared with me about his life in Kathmandu. For myself, I practiced being conscious from moment to moment, being conscious of what it means to live in the paradigm of vulnerability and humility. Adam's missives to me began to change. At first, it was the essence more than the words.

Then, from one moment to the next, he came out of his man-cave and revealed himself. His fears, full-blown and raw, poured out of his heart and smeared blood and tears across the page.

SUBJECT: **In the Man-Cave**

Dearest Kimberley,

I'm so fatigued by thinking and posturing about true love.

This is not easy! My explorations, so far, have introduced me to some of my less desirable prejudices, my base fears…oh…I have a new one…being taken advantage of…I have some nurturing to do for my inner child…he is crying, alone and scared and I need to be with him.

To further your beautifully crafted metaphor:

I am standing at the entrance to the labyrinth…and I see you…I want to come to you, but I have such a long way to go…are you sure you want me to come?

I'm scared to love you…I will be opened like never before…I want to work on myself…and I'm scared…are you a lover or a guide?

I feel I'm from your first paradigm and I'm scared I won't be able to keep up with you as you move to the new paradigm…my negative ego tells me that I won't be able to (not enough earning potential…she will control you…she'll have to pay for you…you'll feel less of a man…etc. etc.)

You are so far ahead of me…my temptation is to retreat from you…slip away and work on myself…go at my own pace and work through my issues in my own time in solitude…if I do this, then it will be okay.

If I don't retreat from you, I feel that I will be in fear of not being enough for you…from the first paradigm, where you are a teacher and me a student…always hoping to prove myself to you…always having a "lack"…I feel cornered in our relationship by my own spirituality, and laboring under the burden of redefining the man I am, to be one with no agendas, "lack" or fears…to the one I want to be.

This quest is a demanding mistress, pushing me to conscious ignorance, and highlighting to me, through your knowledge, my inverse understanding of what true love is…holy %&# Batman! I have tied myself in knots.*

I know you will say that love conquers all…that we will be okay…that we make and create our own reality…that you love me and that I must come "home" to you.

I want you to seriously consider what I have written.

You will know that I'm trying to frighten you…to make you have second thoughts about us…because if you say that's it…then it will relieve me from making a decision about us…it would be easier for me if we ended our relationship, than it would be to continue…as I wouldn't have to face the fact that I have so much to do in so little time to be ready for you in the second paradigm …

This "vulnerability" thing has me spooked…it's not about being a guarded male, as you may surmise…it's about the time I need, to deal with the underlying issues to be ready to love another…to the state of complete surrender…I am concerned that I will in some way be a liability to you, and the impact this feeling will have on me…I am simply not ready!

I'm afraid about committing to the pursuit of absolute vulnerability, even though I know it's the path to true love…dealing with my agendas, and lack (which is not so frightening…but still frightening, if you know what I mean).

Even though I'm afraid…I am going to plunge in! I have decided… but whether we are together? Is it feasible? What feelings do you have? I don't know if I am strong enough…let alone good enough.

I'm still in my man-cave…and tossing the bones and trying to understand this task I have set myself. The one I have decided I will make my life's work…and now dealing with the impact of that decision on us…on the possibility that we can create such beauty and joy.

You may think that I have adopted a victim "oh, woe is me" approach to my conundrum…I thought about that…and I don't believe I am…I am not seeking a comforting and sympathetic arm around my shoulder from you…I am giving you this information so that you have the facts and can decide, from your standpoint, how you feel about dragging a first-paradigm-man into the second, when he is not ready…and has a shitload (Australian term) of work to do…I have reservations…I'll not lie (and most of them are outlined here).

Kimberley, my sweet loving woman…I am confused, doubtful and scared. Your voice will be saying…well…what do you want Adam? The curious answer is…I don't know.

I feel you close to me, my head on your breast…I'm listening to your heart as it beats slowly.

Adam xoxoxo

Adam's email astonished me. It was not the fact that he had these fears, I knew that he did, what astonished me was that he could so boldly and vulnerably tell himself of these fears. I told you he's brilliant. The fact that he could feel his fears and communicate them with such clarity was truly awe-inspiring.

As I read his words and felt his frustration, fear, and pain, I fell more deeply in love with him, even though I knew he was withdrawing. He honestly revealed that he was looking for me to make it "easy" on him by ending the relationship. But, as I shared with Adam, it was the vulnerability in one another that we loved. Adam's vulnerability and fear called to my love and compassion;

my loving Adam, for this new paradigm was not contingent on him loving me back.

Adam's missive was so intricate on so many levels that to do it justice I will have to share it again with you line-by-line, along with my line-by-line reply. Only in this way will you be able to appreciate the depth and complexity playing themselves out in our exchange. Perhaps in doing it this way, you will feel what I felt. Perhaps you will feel what Adam felt. Perhaps you will join us in our dance of vulnerability and humility.

SUBJECT: ***Crawling into the Man-Cave with You***

Hello Love,

Fear and the unknown can be exhausting. It can also give us sleepless nights. I have experienced both in the last few days. You are not lost alone, we are lost…it is up to us if we want to be lost together. You said so much that I am going to comment under your words, so that feelings do not get lost in the translation.

A: "Dearest Kimberley,

I'm so fatigued by thinking and posturing about true love …

This is not easy! My explorations, so far, have introduced me to some of my less desirable prejudices, my base fears…oh…I have a new one…being taken advantage of…I have some nurturing to do for my inner child…he is crying, alone and scared and I need to be with him …"

K: The fact that you see your ugliness and are appalled by it is more than half the journey. Loving and nurturing your child and adolescent is part of self-love.

A: "To further your beautifully crafted metaphor…I am standing at the entrance to the labyrinth…and I see you…I want to come to you, but I have such a long way to go. Are you sure you want me to come?"

K: Oh Adam, in this missive you give me so many opportunities to control and manipulate. I refuse to do that to me, to you, or to us. What I want is not the point. The point is, "What do you want?" I cannot be responsible for your choices. I cannot offer guarantees. Loving is a risk, pure and simple. I all but weep as I write this. From the new paradigm the old one wants to pull me back. I cannot go there. I feel like I am being pulled in two, and then in the next moment I am my new self, solid and true.

A: *"I'm scared to love you…I will be opened like never before…"*

K; And I am scared to love you. Terrified. Will I be trapped? Will you expect from me what I do not want to give? Will you open your heart and really love? Will you blame me if our path ends after we both have opened our hearts? On the other hand, there is a solidity in my belief about my love for you. And, sweetheart, I believe in yours.

A: *"I want to work on myself…and I'm scared…are you a lover or a guide?"*

K: Maybe both lover and guide…as I hope you will be for me. We can take turns offering parts of ourselves that may be more advanced than what the other possesses. More advanced doesn't mean "better than." It does not mean superior. One of the qualities you have, that I admire the most, is your willingness to look at your manhood and what it means to you. What kind of man, not just male, do you want to be? Adam, asking yourself that question is rare and precious. I am putting my face between your neck and shoulder, breathing you into me. I am putting my forehead on your chest and asking for help for us both.

A: *"I feel I'm from your first paradigm, and I'm scared I won't be able to keep up with you as you move to the new paradigm…my negative ego tells me that I won't be able to (not enough earning potential…she will control you…she'll have to pay for you…you'll feel less of a man…etc.)"*

K: You are from my first paradigm. How could you not be scared at what that means? I was in my first paradigm until just days ago…days, hours; not months or years. But I am solidly rooted in my determination to stay here. I will get continued help from my mentor to stay here. I will hold the space for you to join me…but love, that is your decision not mine. Earning potential…sweetheart, be happy…follow your passion…stay on your Soul's path…the abundance always follows.

A: *"You are so far ahead of me…my temptation is to retreat from you…to slip away and work on myself…go at my own pace and work through my issues in my own time in solitude…if I do this then it will be okay…"*

K: Yes, in many ways I am ahead of you in knowledge, and in experience of the type we are talking about. I am not ahead of you in your capacity to love, in your integrity or in your brilliant mind. I feel you slip away…I feel your desire to do so and it breaks my heart…and I have to let you go…if you come to me now it is because you want to, knowing all of this. I want you in my new world, but I do not want you with a kicking and screaming negative ego you do not control. So my love, I release you from all promises. You are now free to slip away or to walk with me.

A: *"If I don't retreat from you, I feel that I will be in fear of not being enough for you…from the first paradigm, where you are a teacher and me a student…always hoping to prove myself to you…always having a lack…I feel cornered in our relationship by my own spirituality and laboring under the burden of redefining the man I am, to be one with no agendas, lack or fears…to the one I want to be…"*

K: The irony is I love you now, just the way you are. You are already magnificent in my eyes. Yes, you have issues to resolve, you know what they are. More, you were on the path of growth when we met. I did not put you on the path, you did. I changed your destiny, that is true. You will always want more for yourself and your life now. You will never again be happy, or even content with a little life. Not when you know greatness is in you. Not when you only need to resolve your personal issues to taste it, and indeed serve the world by being your Truer Self. You changed my destiny as well. I will never again want a man who comes to me to be fixed, or to fill a "lack" in me.

A: *"This quest is a demanding mistress, pushing me to conscious ignorance, and highlighting to me, through your knowledge, my inverse understanding of what true love is…holy %&#@ Batman! I have tied myself in knots…"*

K: So let us look at the truth. You came to explore love—all of it. That starts with self-love. In order to love yourself you must heal your child and adolescent selves. In order to love yourself, you must end the pain others have heaped upon you, and we call that shame. In order to love yourself, you must stop feeling not good enough and know that you are deserving. Sounds like a lot, does it not?

Now think again, after sitting the sneaky bastard, your negative ego, in his chair. You are a loving man and you can easily love your child and adolescent. This is not a burden, but a privilege, that will change your world immediately.

Shame, deservability, and being enough are all tied together. One path will weave easily into the other. Will the work be hard? Yes. Is it worth it? It was for me. I never want to go back and be in that kind of pain again. So your path, my love, the one that you set for yourself, is to love yourself by ending the pain. My gift is the tools with which to do that. That is it. Your gift is much larger…you have to do the work. What is the resistance? Your sneaky bastard, that damn negative ego, does not want you out of pain, because it can manipulate you with the threat of pain. It can control you with the threat of pain.

In your heart of hearts you know this. Because I too had been lost and in terrible pain, I can see the path more clearly than you. It is hard to see the path when you are on it, and not able to see over the next hill. Staying true to our metaphor, you are lost in the labyrinth and from time to time will reach a dead end. Yup, it happens and so what? You backtrack and at the bend you choose another direction. It is life. It is an adventurer's journey. It is what you came here for.

A: *"I know you will say that love conquers all…that we will be okay…that we make and create our own reality…that you love me and that I must come 'home' to you…"*

K: I will not say love conquers all, because it does not. Nor does time heal all wounds. No, we must add intimacy to love. We must add conscious tools of healing to time. Then we can conquer anything. Miracles can happen and magic can abound. My love is for you and does not tie you. Again, my love, be free. Do what you need and want to do. I can pray it is to come home to me, but if not I will love you and see you on your journey. I will cry and mourn and be okay.

A: *"I want you to seriously consider what I have written...you will know that I'm trying to frighten you...to make you have second thoughts about us...because if you say that is it...then it will relieve me from making a decision about us...it would be easier for me...if we ended our relationship, than it would be to continue...as I wouldn't have to face the fact that I have so much to do in so little time to be ready for you in the 2nd paradigm."*

K: Easy is not always the best choice. But Adam, choice is the highest magic. It is as precious a gift as life. Life without choice...well the Goddess herself created choice as her gift. What you choose to do with her two gifts...life and choice... is up to you. For the last two days I have been so lost and so unbalanced, that I could not have written you back as clearly and purely as I can today. Coming out of my woman-cave, and finding you peeking your head out of your cave, is a blessing. You are a blessing, but I only want you if you want me and us.

A: *"This 'vulnerability' thing has me spooked...it's not about being a guarded male, as you may surmise...it's about the time I need to deal with the underlying issues to be ready to love another...to the state of complete surrender...I am concerned that I will in some way be a liability to you, and the impact this feeling will have on me...I am simply not ready!"*

K: I have to wonder when you turned on the stopwatch? Who is watching the clock? What is too long? What does that mean? Yes, now that your path has a map, you jumped in. I so admire that in you. But I do not have a ticking clock. If and when you come back to me, it will be because it is the right thing to do. You are free now. If you want a new commitment, you will ask for it. If you do not, you have someone in the world who loves you and who will be there for you. I want to work on our relationship. I want to love you. But you are correct when you say my love alone is not enough.

A: *"I'm afraid about committing to the pursuit of absolute vulnerability, even though I know it's the path to true love…dealing with my agendas, and lack (which is not so frightening…but still frightening, if you know what I mean?)"*

K: Yes love, I know exactly what you mean. I am so new to this, I can only imagine what it must be like without years of preparation. You are so courageous and I do love you.

A: *"Even though I'm afraid…I am going to plunge in! I have decided…but whether we are together? Is it feasible? What feelings do you have? I don't know if I am strong enough…let alone good enough…"*

K: Of course you are strong enough. That is your sneaky bastard talking. It is choice…do you want to be in love with me? Do you want to create magic together? Do you want to fight with me because that is more fun than "playing" with any other? If you do, you will. The map is there. Read the map. Follow it. What do I feel? I love you. I love you. And I love me. I am staying in the new paradigm. I hope you choose to join me. I hope you choose to love me. But if you do not, I will not love you any less. It takes more than love, it takes intimacy, it takes honesty, it takes commitment and sometimes just plain old hard work. Am I willing? Oh yes. Am I scared? Nope, I am terrified.

A: *"I'm still in my man-cave…and tossing the bones and trying to understand this task I have set myself…the one I have decided I will make my life's work…and now dealing with the impact of that decision on us…on the possibility that we can create such beauty and joy …"*

K: It is this possibility that fills me with such magical hope. Growth is our life's work. Being of service on the planet is our life's work. Can we do it together? Yes...will we? Choice.

A: "*You may think that I have adopted a victim 'oh, woe is me' approach to my conundrum...I thought about that... and I don't believe I am...I am not seeking a comforting and sympathetic arm around my shoulder from you...I am giving you this information so that you have the facts and can decide, from your standpoint, how you feel about dragging a first-paradigm-man into the second when he is not ready...and has a shitload (Australian term) of work to do...I have reservations...I'll not lie (and most of them are outlined here)...*"

K: No, I never once thought anything you have expressed was as a victim. My arms around you will offer comfort, but not from pity, rather from compassion. I am not dragging you, nor will I. I remind you: you chose this path. You created me in your life to make the path easier, because I have a map through my mentors. I know you doubt yourself. That will pass as you deal with your Shame, etc. You do not know what you want for us. I understand that. I know we have to begin again or not at all. I think this love missive is beginning again. It is a love missive, because in truth lies love. Let me introduce myself: my name is Kimberley. Somewhere in the world is a man I love. He is not committed to me. He is committed to his growth. He has not yet decided about us. I do not know if I will ever see him again. I do know I love him and no matter where he goes he will have someone, somewhere in the world, who loves him. No strings. No promises. Just love. See? Choice.

A: "*Kimberley, my sweet loving woman...I am confused, doubtful and scared...your voice will be saying...well...what do you want, Adam?...the curious answer is...I don't know...I feel you close to me, my head on your breast...I'm listening to your heart as it beats slowly..."*

K: Yes my love, I will hold you close no matter what you decide. I honor you and admire you.

Kimberley

As I gift you with the unveiling of Adam's and my dance of love, the same song lyric keeps going though my head...*"Love is what we came here for."* What I did not realize until now, and what Adam did not realize, was that the first love is to self. My missive of love in response to Adam's bravery and courage, was one of self-love.

Adam did try to scare me into running from him and his fears. His self-admitted ploy did not work. I loved myself enough to consciously choose what I wanted. I had changed enough to hold my boundaries. I was in a new paradigm with new beliefs firmly in place.

I loved Adam and that meant I wanted him to know he was free. All of the promises we made from the old paradigm were released. Adam and I had to find our way back through the labyrinth to each other, or not. This journey of self-love, belief changing, and vulnerability was, and would continue to be, a conscious choice for both of us.

CHAPTER NINE:

18 Days, 2 Hrs, 8 Mins

FEAR IS A PART of life. When our beliefs do not work for us, fear can rapidly escalate into terror. Each of us has developed patterns of dealing with fear: denial, avoidance, anger, rage, stagnation, self-abuse, substance abuse, self-abandonment, self-pity and refusal to risk love are but a few.

Adam and I both had come to the place where we could use the energy of fear to propel us forward into love and growth, or we could use that same fear to pull back and succumb. No one could make the choice for us. Adam had to choose for himself, as did I.

Adam and I, one dark night, wrote of our fear of risking love:

SUBJECT: **FEAR**

Hello gorgeous woman…it's the basket case!

I feel much better from reading your email to me…I will feel like this until I am ready to commit to you and …

Then I will be well on the path! I'm still in the cave…but I am structuring my task and I'm optimistic that I will know my path to true love …

I thank you for your patience...I am most thankful for the beautiful woman you are, and that you are here...with me...in my life, holding my hand and resting with me :-)

Don't think for a minute I am not aware of your pain caused by my hesitancy in letting my heart go free with you...I am also in pain because of this...this is perhaps where my stopwatch comes from...it's actually not on you...or us...but it's on me...I have realized this...I thought it was you who was pressuring me to make decisions...but it's not...I realize it is a lifetime, that it will take me to understand and love openly, fully, with supreme intimacy and vulnerability...including continued work, (as I'm sure I will change and the task will always be here) ...

For me it's not a quick jump from the first to the second paradigm...who was I kidding? You say you have been preparing for this for decades...and were able to make the transition because you were ready. I've been asleep for a long time.

I think this is my third task...it certainly is a worthy one ...

You have been gracious, beautifully feminine, and loving whilst watching me take my feet off the tightrope one at a time...become unsettled, panic, scared myself and retreat... FEAR! If I'm not aware of it...fear will surround me in a mist so thick, I will not be able to move...and I will not be able to see you in the labyrinth...let alone find my way to you ...

I again ask you for your love and patience as I toss the bones in my cave...posturing this way and that...wrestling with my negative ego, nurturing my Self, re-discovering my masculine and coming to life from my heart...I used to think I was the one who always held the space for others...but now I am asking you...I need this...your love soothes me ...

My initial quest for my truth, clarity of purpose, and perspective on life has become absorbed within a question of knowing "true love"...instead of being main drivers for me, they are but internal supporting walls to the pinnacle of my existence...love.

This much I know.

What I also know is that whether you be lover or guide (or both), you have had a profound affect on me, my being, and as you said...my destiny. I do know your heart is pure and I revel in the fact that you will sit in the fire with me and are not afraid...it is a mutual appreciation society here...as I too think you are extraordinary...xoxoxo

Anyway gorgeous...I feel your presence all around me...I am truly blessed :-) xoxoxoxo

Adam

SUBJECT: **Re: FEAR**

It is about 4 a.m. your time and I hope you are fast asleep.

My mentor and I spoke this morning about us. I told him I set you free and that I really wanted your happiness. This is so true for me, that I am proud of myself. I can honestly love you without expectation of you. Oh yes, there are times I am in pain. When I am in pain, I am mourning the loss of the possibility of us. In the old paradigm, possibilities were limited because it was packed with agendas for both of us. Will there be possibilities in the new paradigm for us? You haven't yet decided.

I feel the fear of that and know I have to walk through that fear, or be damaged by it, including any possibility of us. So, meditatively, I went to the new paradigm today. In order to get to that place of clarity and wholeness I had to walk though my own fears. What I know about fear, is that walking into it is the only way through it. Every time I put my toe in and get scared, and consequently pull back, I prolong the fear. So even though I was surrounded in dark, black fog, I kept feeling and walking. It began like this. I (metaphors now) began on a ship. I am such a buccaneer (positive pirate). On that ship my lesser self was pacing. Back and forth. Back and forth. She did not want me to get off the ship and step on new land or into the new world. Her fear and anxiety was intense. She brought reinforcements to convince me not to risk. She brought the bully, the controller in me. He was big and brutish. She brought the whiny self-pitying me. Those three were easy to speak with. The one that surprised me was a rabid child-self. Holy smokes, huge teeth and too many of them. This was the part that wanted to intimidate me into "staying safe." She was the one who defended my old beliefs about love.

I told all of them that they did not have to go with me. In fact they had no place in the new paradigm. Once they knew they did not have to go and that I would be back and give them what they need (unconditional love), they all stood at the rail watching me leave.

I started to row to shore when a black fog of fear surrounded me. I wanted to "see" where I was going, and in order to do that I had to row moving my arms in the opposite direction to how one normally rows...facing with my back to the front...I see this as a wonderful metaphor for how to get to the new world, the new paradigm. Change my beliefs and change my reality...the old ones do not work for me.

The old ways do not work. How I always did things does not work. So, I rowed sitting forward. Once on shore I walked into the fog. I couldn't see a bloody thing. Another metaphor, fear so often blinds me. Rather than sit in the fog of fear, I risked moving deeper into it. I was frightened, but not terrified. I moved forward. It seemed to take a long time. Step after step. I kept hoping that soon I would be out of the fear. I could feel how afraid I was of the unknown, of this new paradigm. But I was not willing to go back.

Finally, I came to a place of purity. It was a small grotto with a waterfall. There were a few big rocks in the smallish pond, into which the waterfall descended and it was surrounded by trees. I have been there once in this reality and it was a place of magnificence and gentle beauty. There was nothing I could see from this place. It was totally surrounded by the fog. Not as if I was boxed in, but rather as if I had not yet created anything beyond this place of purity.

That, my love, is what it feels like to walk through the fear. Sometimes it seems like I will never come out the other side. For me, the only choice is to brave it and keep walking. No matter how many times I stumble in the dark, I will not go back.

I know there is always a place of beauty waiting for me when I destroy old beliefs that do not work. And I know I create a new world every time I create a new belief.

Right beyond the oasis of magnificence and gentle beauty is my world, waiting for what I will fashion next. What will I create with my new beliefs?

Dream well My Love,

K

Adam told me repeatedly that love was his life's mission. As he sat in his man-cave only he could decide if that mission of love included us. He knew he had to face and change his beliefs. He knew he had to learn to change what was once true, based on his old beliefs, about women, about love, and about himself.

One day, not long after he began to look at his beliefs, he wrote:

SUBJECT: ***It is ME***

This shit…is about me…not you or us…but me…F#&!*

I just wrote in my journal that…"I will take full responsibility for everything I think, do, and feel!"

F#&ing negative ego!*

Adam

These short sentences, expletives and all, gave me hope. Adam really saw that he was the captain of his own ship. He got that it was his beliefs that stood in the way. So he did the only reasonable thing; he reached out for help and asked how to change his beliefs.

So I shared with Adam the steps of changing beliefs, and then I stepped back. I could not be his mentor or his guide in this. This was a journey he needed to do without me. Yet, we all initially need help walking the steps of change. I have had plenty of help, so I shared with him the name of a loving friend who could help.

You and I, however, can walk the steps of permanent change together. As we do, I will continue to share with you Adam's and my journey of love. As I do, notice that we both grow, but do we both change? Growth and change are different processes and should not be confused. Only change can create long-lasting differences in us. We can continue to grow by developing insight and accumulating knowledge. However, this new insight and knowledge does not guarantee a difference in our behavior, or in how we feel. Growth prepares us to change, it is not the change. In part two, ***The Story of Change,*** you and I will journey together. We will learn how to create more than growth—we will learn how to change.

PART TWO:

THE STORY OF CHANGE

CHAPTER TEN:

Recognize

4 STEPS TO THE LOVE OF YOUR LIFE

PAIN AND FEAR often catapult us into a desire to grow. We want to get out of the pain and fear, so we are often more willing to risk growth and even change. As I mentioned, growth and change are not the same. Together, in this part of the book, we will walk through the steps of what to change, and how to change.

Contrary to what most people think, we do not have to wait for pain or fear in order to grow or change. We can allow love to be our reason to risk change. Adam and I wrestled with our willingness to change, and love was the reason. Most of us dislike change and will do almost anything to delay or eliminate the need for it. Change makes us uncomfortable; all you have to do is read our missives and you will see how uncomfortable change can be.

We, as a society, falsely believe that permanent change only happens after some awful heart-ripping event. It is true that we can use pain as our impetus to change, and most people do. But, it is not true that this is the best path to permanent change.

I believe that love for *ourselves* is the best reason to risk change.

Truly loving *ourselves* gives us the courage to risk the chaos that is the outcome of change. Why chaos? Because we have to discover who we are in the world once we have changed. Remember Adam's revelation:

"This shit…is about me…not you or us…but me…Fu#&!"

Change always starts within us, for us, by us—but we do not have to walk the steps of change alone. We do not have to discover the secrets to more elegant change by ourselves. We can, and should, get help. So, let's walk the four steps of change together.

How to Change Anything You Want: The Change Process[2]

I learned this process from my friend and mentor, Lazaris. He has blessed tens of thousands of lives, including mine, by showing us how to access our subconscious mind and how to work with it to change.

The process has four steps:

Step 1: Recognize

Step 2: Acknowledge

Step 3: Forgive

Step 4: Change

That's it, four steps to changing your life. Four steps to getting the love of your life. Truly, this is how it works. The only question is: are you willing to do the work it takes to change? For me, the answer was yes. Adam, as he worked in his man-cave, was very willing to grow, and was still deciding if he would risk change.

The four steps are complex, yet can be accomplished with ease. How easy or difficult the process is depends on how hard you struggle against it. Adam tied himself in knots in his man-cave. You can feel his frustration, his pain, and you can taste his resistance. My heart bled for him, but only he could face down his resistance to change. The same is true for me and for you.

For me it became a choice between staying in an old paradigm and a way of being in the world that did not work for me, or risk change.

Does your life work for you the way you hoped it would? If the answer, in any arena (love, money, career, self-love, etc.,) is NO, then you are at the crossroads. Will you risk change? If you are willing, let's walk the path together, four steps to a new future.

The first step is to ***Recognize*** that you want to change. For you, that might seem obvious; it was for me. I knew I wanted more from my life than I had. I knew I wanted to reach for "being" more. Take a moment, and consider that we are talking about permanent change. You have read our missives; you know I was committed to the permanent change of living in my new paradigm of vulnerability, humility, and intimacy even if that meant losing Adam. Why would I risk permanent change that could destroy the magic and love between Adam and myself? Because to do anything less would be to destroy me. To do anything less would mean disavowing the covenant I had made to always reach for the "more" of me.

To embrace permanent change, we have to know what beliefs we want to change. This is not a discussion about changing your life circumstance rather it is about changing you, which in turn will change your life.

This first step takes a commitment from you. Are you willing to look into yourself and see yourself? Is love a big enough motivator for you? It was for me. Step one is almost too obvious; in order to change you must ***Recognize*** what it is that needs changing. You have to do the work to discover the belief(s) that are in your way, the belief(s) that keep you from the love you so richly deserve.

Step 1: Recognize–Our Beliefs Create Our Experiences

Twenty years before I met Adam, I remember feeling as lost as he was. And, just as he shared his awakening with me, I share mine with you. My awakening began one misty, Friday night in Mill Valley, California, when I first heard of an innovative concept about beliefs and belief systems.

I was attending a weekend personal-growth seminar and the speaker said something amazing: "Your beliefs create your experiences." The impact of those words was immediate. I felt a dull thud in my abdomen as the words reached my conscious mind.

The implications of that statement were staggering. When the statement was made again—"Your beliefs create your experiences"—it hit me with full force. In fact, I was so intrigued by this statement, that those exact words continued to reverberate in my mind during the entire presentation.

Later, as I watched tendrils of fog invade the San Francisco Bay from my hotel window, I thought about those words again. I wondered if my perception of life might be much like this fog. How quickly the fog had engulfed the bay, hiding even the brightest city lights. Had the beliefs I embraced so dearly all my life acted in the same way, blinding me to a new reality?

My mind continued to race. If my beliefs truly did create my experiences, I would have to rethink my entire life. Like most of us, I had always been taught the complete opposite: that my experiences created my beliefs. Now, I was presented with a new way of thinking. I began to wonder if my beliefs could, indeed, create my experiences. I fumbled through a maze of examples, trying to make sense of one theory or the other. The pieces churned round and round. Sometimes they seemed to fit; other times they did not. Slowly, I began to realize that perhaps the pieces did not need to fit together immediately for me.

Rather then demand that I totally understand the concept immediately maybe it would be better if I explored my beliefs and determined if they matched the reality of my life. So I began the journey and like Adam stumbled, fell, resisted and then discovered the truth, my beliefs create my experience. This new awareness was both powerful and frightening. And with it came total freedom embraced by total responsibility.

If I, indeed, created my world based on my beliefs, then any experience I have ever had was created by me. Remember Adam's words, "*It is about me! Not you or us.*" My thoughts went in a similar vein. I realized in the long-ago hotel room in San Francisco that I, alone, was responsible for what I had created. It also meant I had the freedom to create whatever I chose to believe. Perhaps this is what Anaïs Nin[3] felt when she wrote, and I paraphrase:

> *So, the day I was told by* Otto Rank *[her psychotherapist in the 1930s] that I was responsible for the failures, the defeats that had happened to me, and that it was in my power to conquer them, that day was a very exhilarating day. Because if you're told that you're responsible that means that you can do something about it. Whereas the people who say society is responsible, or some of the feminist women who say man is responsible, there is nothing you can do. I preferred to take the blame, because that also means that one can act, and it's such a relief from passivity, from being the victim.*

Secret: ***It is our beliefs that create reality.***

Getting What You Want

Isn't that what it's all about—getting what we want? Isn't that why you're reading this book to get what you want, the love of your life? Just from the heading of this section alone, you might think, "Oh, the good part. Now she is going to tell me how to do it—how to get what I want."

Well, I would like to suggest that we already have what we want. Just as Adam and I had what we really wanted—you have what you really want. "We don't always get what we ask for, but we always get what we want." That was another profound tidbit from that foggy day in San Francisco. That's right: we already have exactly what we want in our lives at this very moment. Maybe we didn't ask for it consciously, but some part of us (our subconscious mind) knows, based on our beliefs, what we really want.

Of course, this only makes sense if we remember our initial premise: our beliefs create our experiences. "We have what we want" means that we have what we believe is possible, and what we believe we deserve.

Adam believed that, "women betray." Consequently, when I lied by omission, not telling him my age, for him that was a betrayal. Adam, by having the belief "woman betray" will have to, by virtue of how beliefs work, create a woman who he experiences as betraying. There is no way around our beliefs. They are hard-wired into us and unless we change them they will always be honored. If Adam believes women betray, he will create betrayal.

For myself, my old belief that "*no man will love me in the way I want*," meant that no matter how magnificent the man I created, he will on some level, not love me in the way I wanted.

Because you, me, Adam, indeed everyone, has never been taught to distinguish the difference between what we think and what we believe, most of us are outraged by the statements "we have the love life we really want," and "we have in our lives what we really want." We think we want all sorts of things we do not have; learning that we already have what we really want may not only sound untrue, it may sound incredibly unfair.

Believing Can Make it So

Beliefs are an immense power in our lives because they are the prime creators of our experiences. You can clearly see that from Adam and me. Can you see it in yourself? However, there are also other influencers of how we experience realities, such as our attitudes, thoughts, feelings, decisions, and choices.

For example, we have been told repeatedly to think positively. Why? Because what and how we think actually does affect what happens around us, and how other people respond to us. Yet, if thinking creates our reality, why don't all our thoughts manifest themselves? Because the reality our thinking creates, ultimately honors our belief systems. The same is true of our attitudes, feelings, decisions, and choices. They can only support a reality that is within the parameters of our beliefs. Beliefs are one of the major powers in our lives. This is the reason some of our thoughts, such as "I found the perfect love," might not become a reality, if our belief is "love hurts." Our thoughts will ultimately be overridden by our beliefs.

Let's take this further and look more deeply at how these all work independently and together to influence our reality by honoring our beliefs. As I mentioned these elements are attitudes, thoughts, feelings, decisions, and choices. By placing these elements in a diagram, perhaps it will be easier to understand the relationship each of these has to the other.

Since this is a complex concept to grasp, let's picture it like this: think of a wheel. The hub of the wheel represents our beliefs. The spokes work independently and together to support the outer rim, which represents our experiences or reality. Let's take a closer look at each spoke in our wheel of reality in order to see how each works to create experiences that honors the hub: our beliefs.

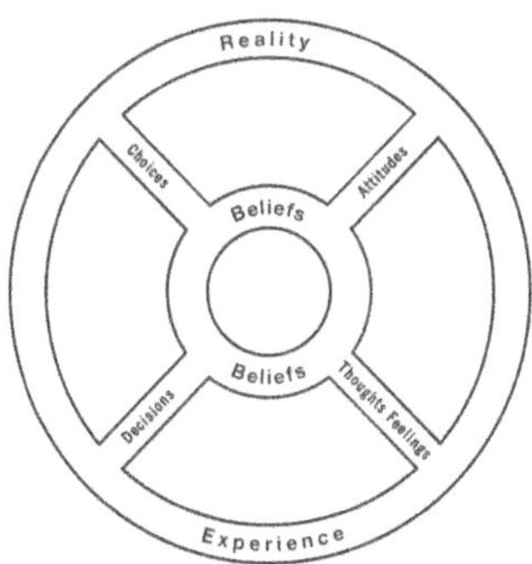

Our attitudes are perhaps best described as the color we paint our world. Our attitudes color or prejudice everything we experience. Two people can have identical beliefs (e.g., "love hurts"), yet their individual attitudes can create totally different experiences in the world.

For example, the attitude of one person who believes "love hurts" might be that "this is just how life is and therefore I must learn to survive and do the best I can." Consequently, this person's attitude will help create experiences that make the best of a bad thing. Though the belief is "love hurts," the attitude allows the creation of a more positive reality from that constricting belief, than would have otherwise been possible.

On the other hand, the attitude of another person having the identical belief, "love hurts," might have the attitude that, "the world has a personal vendetta against me." Consequently, this person may create embittered and hateful experiences to honor the belief that "love hurts." Clearly, individual attitudes can create different life experiences based upon the same belief.

Thoughts are also powerful influencers, as are feelings. Each thought and feeling we have creates a flow of energy that can be consciously utilized to enhance or inhibit our lives. Learning how to use these energies is a skill that would serve us well to develop. For instance, if we are angry, that is simply a normal human emotion or feeling. What we do with the energy generated by our anger helps influence our reality. Following our example, "love hurts," when that belief is manifested by love hurting us, as it must, what we do with the anger around the hurt helps dictate how we experience life. We can use the anger to hurt and punish ourselves or others, or allow it to catapult us over obstacles. In short, we can use the feeling "anger" in a constricting way to hurt others, or in an expansive way as a motivator over life's hurdles.

We can also learn to harness the energy of our thoughts. We can use the energy created by a thought ("I can do anything I want with my life") to influence the reality we create for ourselves, either positively or negatively.

Our decisions are strongly influenced by our attitudes, thoughts, and feelings. The variety of choices we allow ourselves is also based on these factors. However, the final choices we make are influenced by all the above factors, including our decisions. For instance, if we only allow ourselves the choice between a "hurt-filled relationship" or "no relationship," we might well make the final choice of having no relationship. It is choice that holds the highest power of all of these: attitude, thoughts, feelings, and decisions. Once again, viewing the wheel, you see that all of these: attitude, thoughts, feelings, decisions, and choices originate from our beliefs. They are influencers and sometimes creators. Yet anything they create must be in alignment with our belief, or the creation will not hold.

Have you ever wondered how something that you worked for, dreamt about, and finally created, just slipped through your fingers? That wonderful thing that you created was not supported by your beliefs, so no matter how much you wanted it, it would disappear. More times than not, you had no idea why it disappeared, or perhaps you came up with factors you used to reconcile the loss. The core truth is that anything you want in your life must be supported by your beliefs! No matter how great your attitude, how in alignment your thoughts and feelings, and how many well thought out decisions and ultimately, great choices you made, if they are not in sync with your beliefs, it will all come crashing down on top of you.

Secret: ***Change your beliefs, change your life.***

This explains why therapy does not always create permanent change. Changing attitudes, thoughts, feelings, decisions, and/or choices results in a job half done. Finally, we understand it is our beliefs that must be changed in order to create and sustain permanent change.

The Subconscious Mind

Now that we know that our beliefs, along with support from our attitudes, thoughts, feelings, decisions, and choices, create our reality, let's take a look at how that happens.

We have three minds: the conscious, subconscious and unconscious. The one we will be investigating is our much-maligned subconscious mind. In truth, it is a faithful servant who has done exactly what we have asked for our entire lives.

Our subconscious mind is key in creating our reality because it is the storehouse of our beliefs and more, its phenomenal power ensures that those beliefs are played out in life. Our subconscious mind makes sure that our reality always reflects the beliefs we have stored within it. In order to understand how this works, let's try visualizing our subconscious as a huge mainframe computer.

Like all computers, our subconscious mind does exactly what we ask it to do. It has two major jobs or functions: to store information, including all our beliefs; and to create a reality that honors those beliefs.

Job One: Our subconscious mind stores all the information we encounter. This means absolutely every bit of information—from every street sign we might have read to every dream we ever had, even the ones we think we don't remember. It stores, and holds as sacred, all of the beliefs and information we have created. Our subconscious mind stores all this information, saving us the task of having to be consciously aware of everything we know. To better comprehend the enormity of this, imagine memorizing every book in the Library of Congress and keeping all that information current. This is the type of work our subconscious mind does, thus leaving us energy for other, more important, tasks.

Job Two: Our subconscious mind creates experiences in our lives that honor the beliefs we have given it. Our subconscious mind interprets our beliefs as sacrosanct orders, as if we are its god. Our subconscious honors our beliefs, and has no ability to judge or evaluate them. For instance, Adam does not consciously want women to betray him, yet in his experience they all do. His belief that "women betray" is programmed into his internal computer, into his subconscious mind. Nothing he does, until he changes that belief, will ever change his experiences of women. His subconscious mind does not consider the untold pain of this belief, it just simply obeys its programming. The computer in your phone, on your desk and in your briefcase, has no opinion about what is programmed there. Nor does it have the ability to care about frustration or pain that programming might cause. It simply follows its orders —our orders. It obeys us absolutely. This is how our subconscious mind works.

Secret ***Our subconscious mind stores our beliefs and makes sure they are honored in our life experiences.***

As we live from moment to moment, our subconscious mind makes sure that our beliefs are honored. It is like the hub in our wheel—our beliefs. The phenomenal energy of our subconscious mind, not unlike gravity, pulls anything that honors our beliefs into our reality.

For instance, let's go back to an earlier example: "love hurts." The hub of the wheel is the belief "love hurts." As the wheel spins, its gravitational force pulls in and holds corresponding attitudes, thoughts, feelings, decisions, and choices.

1. Attitudes: the opposite sex cannot be trusted.

2. Thoughts: every relationship I have ever had ended badly.
3. Feelings: I feel hurt.
4. Decisions: to have no relationship or one that is hurtful.
5. Choices: I choose not to be in romantic relationships.

If any element that does not honor the belief tries to attach to the hub, that element will be crushed by the force of the other elements that are attracted by the belief. For example, if Adam had a thought such as "This woman can be trusted," and it tries to attach itself to the hub and consequently become part of his reality, the other elements will override the thought, never allowing it to take hold for any length of time. Because the thought was never allowed to secure itself to the hub of the wheel, its influence will never manifest itself in Adam's reality.

Our subconscious mind stores our beliefs and creates the energy and circumstances to guarantee that our beliefs are ultimately honored in our reality. It also accesses and utilizes our attitudes, thoughts, feelings, decisions and choices to continually create a reality that honors the beliefs it stores.

The Subconscious in Action

How do we know what we actually believe? How do we tap into, or gain access to our subconscious mind to find the beliefs we have stored there? A good place to start is by looking candidly at what you enviably create in a romantic relationship. If women always leave you, ask yourself questions around abandonment, trust and being good enough. Examine your thoughts about women. If men will not commit, look to questions around your feelings of deserving love, anger at men and look to your self-worth.

To help you learn how to think about this, let's turn once again to Adam and me. We both had beliefs that did not work for us. We both needed to look more closely at our constricting beliefs. To do this we had to question what we had created. This time let's look at me, and the questions I had to ask myself.

First look at the reality. The reality I had created was the most openly loving man I had ever had in my life. I loved him. He, in a matter of a few short weeks, went from jumping into our relationship heart first, to locking himself away in his man-cave questioning his love for me, and his worthiness of my love. What beliefs must be in my way to create this kind of reality?

Yes, I changed paradigms and that played a big part in Adam's and my love story. But just as important were our beliefs. During the intensive, my mentor and I reprogrammed my subconscious mind. We changed my beliefs. What questions did I need to ask myself to see if my beliefs around love and relationships worked for me? The same types of questions that may aid you in your search for the love of your life.

To make it easier, you and I will journey the path of growth together. That growth can lead to change. I call these adventures that can lead to growth and change *Homegrowths*.

Homegrowth 1: Looking for the Questions

1. Make a list of questions that will help you gain insight into your true desires regarding a romantic relationship.

   EXAMPLE:

   1. What do I lose by having a romantic relationship?
   2. Will I risk being totally authentic and allowing the woman/man to love the real me?
   3. Am I willing to be loved? (This question stems from the pre-intensive belief, "*No man will love me in the way I want to be loved.*")

2. Answer each question in depth:
   a. Take the time to really think and feel about what questions you need to ask yourself, in order to ferret out answers that can change you.
   b. Think and feel about the answer just as thoroughly.

To help you get the idea about working with the *Homegrowth* exercises, I will review my answers to the questions used in the example.

What Do I Lose by Having a Romantic Relationship?

This is an old question for me. As I explored it anew, I was delighted to find that I no longer feared losing myself. I had changed this belief in the past, and it had held. Once, I actually believed I would love a man so deeply that I would be willing to give up everything I was, just to be with him. I had seen many women, including my own mother, do this. I had read countless books, in which it was imperative for the heroine to give up her own life for the sake of her true love. I had learned the lessons of our culture well: a woman in love should be willing to sacrifice everything for love. I must confess a tiny part of me thought this was terribly romantic. Now I know it's just crap.

Asking myself the question revealed that the internal war that was once a part of every relationship was gone. I did not lose myself to Adam, nor did I want him to lose himself to me. I don't want the burden of being all things to one person. First, it is not possible. Secondly, that would create a co-dependence that would destroy any possibility of the type of relationship I was finally ready to create. Asking the questions revealed a new truth. One I relished. The work of changing my beliefs around romantic relationships in the past had held, and had changed me. They changed me enough so that I could create Adam in my life.

Will I Risk Being Totally Authentic, Allowing a Man to Love the Real Me?

I am a powerful woman. The myth in our society, spread by women, is that men do not want a powerful woman as their love mate. This myth is insulting to men. I must confess I once believed it. As I explored my thoughts I realized that, because I once believed it, consequently I created men that did not want me to be as powerful as I am. Just as importantly I, without being asked, held back my power so I wouldn't overwhelm them. It was my belief that attracted men like that, not men in general.

As I worked this through, I realized I was once the one who did not want to be accountable for my true power: vulnerability, humility, tenderness and intimacy. I had faced those fears in the intensive with my mentor and came triumphantly out the other side of fear. I shifted those beliefs. As I told Adam, I now understood that vulnerability is power and beauty combined. When Adam and I began, I was as authentic as I knew how to be. Mere weeks later, I was different and aimed to be even more authentic. I would be even more vulnerable, tender and humble. I would be even more powerful and more loving. All this is possible because my mentor and I "rewired me" by significantly changing my beliefs.

Relationships have a funny way of reflecting back to us what we need to learn. Being in a relationship is the fastest way to learn what needs to be healed inside of us. Healthy relationships also have a funny way of demanding that we recognize who we really are. I like who I see now when I look in the mirror. That makes all the work worthwhile.

Am I Willing to Be Loved?

This is perhaps one of the most important questions that any of us can ask ourselves. The knee-jerk reaction is to say, "Well duh, what am I doing here if not to learn how to create the love I always wanted?" Ok, now that that is out of your system, take another look. I did.

Adam and I are a miracle. Everything fits. The timing is right, the connection explosive, the intimacy as intense as I have ever created, the communication second to none, our cultures and passion for service matches. I love him. You have read his love missives...do you believe he loves me? Everything works...yet he is in his man-cave trying to decide if being loved by me is right. He is trying to decide, after all of this, if he truly loves me.

This is the reality I created. No one else—me. I could, if I was ignorant enough to do so, blame Adam. But I know better. If Adam, when he comes out of his man-cave, decides that loving me is not right for him, then whose beliefs are in the way? As I have said repeatedly, I will not be a victim. If life—if love!—is not working the way I want it to, I *must* look to myself for the causes and the answers.

I create my own reality, all of it. When Adam loves me, I create that. If he chooses not to love me, then that is my creation as well. If I refuse to look at the question, "Am I willing to be loved?" then I am choosing to be a victim just as Anaïs Nin said. I create my own reality and if that means looking again and again at my beliefs around love, then that is a noble task.

I started to change as soon as Adam and I began our journey into love. Before our journey I might have answered this question, "Am I willing to be loved?" differently. Change works that way. Those of us on that path are ever changing, ever becoming more. So my answer today is yes! I am willing to receive love, first and foremost from myself. I will set boundaries that honor the woman that I am. I will freely give my love. I will risk being more and more loving. When I do, I risk receiving more and more love. Now here is the tricky part, I must be rigorously honest with myself when I say "no" to love. I must question the reasons behind the "no." Sometimes, in the moment, I may not know the why, but if I love myself I must trust that I will discover the answer.

Saying "yes" to love is a life-long journey of exploration. I do not think we will ever know all there is to know about love. I enjoy, most of the time, being on the path of discovering all the aspects of love.

If Adam comes out of his cave and chooses not to love me I will let him go, mourn and heal the loss. I can now do all of these things with seeming ease, because I love myself.

Yes, I am Willing to Be Loved

Exploring new, more honest questions helped me focus on myself and my belief systems. This, of course, was key to shifting paradigms—absolute honesty with myself. Instead of asking a question that denoted blame or judgment, such as "How could Adam love me so beautifully and then just stop?" Instead, I asked questions that helped me probe the inner workings of my subconscious, questions that led me closer to my beliefs.

I think you will be pleasantly surprised to learn that your beliefs are actually quite accessible. As you explore your questions, the answers will open up even more questions, which, in turn, will enable you to look even deeper within yourself. Consider continuing to increase your list with questions such as:

1. Am I willing to take responsibility for my beliefs concerning romantic relationships?
2. Am I willing to take responsibility for all that has happened in my life? Will I set myself free of my past by owning and changing the beliefs that no longer serve me?
3. Am I willing to embrace new beliefs and create a different reality? Am I willing to be different when it might mean letting go of some of the relationships I create from the "old me"?

Secret: ***Since our beliefs create our experience, our reality, we only have to notice what we have (or do not have) in our life to determine what we actually believe.***

Ever since I learned this lesson, my life has become a more open book, constantly displaying my beliefs to me, and this was never more clear and real as with my unfolding relationship with Adam. You now know how to begin to think about beliefs. Let's narrow it down, and choose one belief that you really want to change.

Homegrowth 2: Discovering the Belief I Want to Change.

In this exercise, we are dealing with your subconscious mind—not your thoughts. The key to the success of this exercise is spontaneity. This means answering each blank in one second or less. Yes, one second!

Secret: ***You are not interested in what you think about love, you want to know what you have programmed into your subconscious mind about love.***

That is why you need to respond in less than one second. Any longer and your brain will have time to engage, and you will then simply reveal to yourself what you already consciously know. This exercise is designed to short-circuit your *thinking* by not giving you the time to think. Your subconscious will release the information to you, if you do not allow your *thinking* to get in the way.

Once you get the knack, you will be able to recognize when you move out of spontaneity and begin to *think*.

It is important to complete the exercise in the two-part process as described, as this fosters a deeper level of communication with your subconscious. As with all *Homegrowths*, these responses are for you alone; no one else need ever see them. So be gentle with yourself; try not to judge or censor your responses. Allow the flow of spontaneous communication to create impeccable honesty with yourself.

If you can comfortably do so, work this process with a friend. They can help hold you to the less than one-second time limit, and help you stay focused, should you get frustrated.

1. Choose a category on which to focus. In order to create the love of your life, do you need to change your beliefs around women, men, love, sex, or perhaps your beliefs about yourself? The truth is you may have to work at each of these categories. But for clarity, we will choose just one, and that is love.

   On the far left-hand side of a sheet of paper number from 1 to 33. Starting with the number one write your answer to, "Love Is _____." Write a one-word response. Repeat to yourself again and again very rapidly, "Love is…, Love is…, Love is…," and when the answers start to come, write them down. When you stall, and you will, pull your focus back, clear your mind, and try again. If you get stuck, then put away the exercise for a while. Come back sometime later and continue with your list. Yes, you need to have all 33 responses.

EXAMPLE: Love Is …

Love is hurtful
Love is fun
Love is foolish
Love is wonderful
Love is finite
Love is scary
Love is painful

After you have completed thirty-three one-word responses to "Love Is..." return to the top of the page.

2. Complete each sentence by adding, "and I feel ________." Use the same spontaneous response method described above.

EXAMPLE: Love Is ...

Love is hurtful and I feel angry
Love is fun and I feel happy
Love is foolish and I feel frustrated
Love is wonderful and I feel joyous
Love is finite and I feel hopeless
Love is scary and I feel angry
Love is painful and I feel frightened

Take a close look at your list and decide which beliefs no longer serve you, and which beliefs do you want to change? Notice that many of your beliefs already work for you. Make a list of the top five that do not. Choose one to change as we continue this journey. Let's change it together.

Key Secret: *You only have to look at your life to know what you believe.*

Compare your life experience, with the beliefs you have discovered. They should align. If they do not, you need to re-evaluate your answers or your honesty about your life. If they do, by this comparison you will know exactly what beliefs to change. For instance if you wrote, "Love is painful," you carry the belief somewhere in your subconscious that love hurts. You only need to look at your past relationships to know that is what you create—love hurting. You have also learned how you *feel* about your beliefs. By honestly completing the Homegrowth, you have given yourself vital information. You have now completed the first of the four steps, ***Recognize.***

The first step in changing anything in your life is to ***Recognize*** what belief you want to change. Congratulations! You have done that.

Homegrowth 3: Choose and Grow

In this Homegrowth you will delineate exactly which belief you want to change and what you want to change it to.

1. Choose the one belief you want to change and write it on a separate sheet of paper.
2. Below the belief you want to change, write the new belief you would like to change it to.

Use the same grammatical form or syntax as the original belief, when you create the wording of your new belief. Imagine you are taking a circuit out of a computer. To replace it, you need to use the same size circuit in order for it to fit into the empty slot.

> **Secret:** ***It is not necessary to change the wording of the new belief to the exact opposite of the belief you want to change. You can change the belief to anything you want as long as it "fits" into the space. In other words, as long as you use the same syntax as the belief you are destroying.***

EXAMPLE: Love Is …

Old belief: Love is scary.	New belief: My love is safe.
Old belief: Love hurts.	New belief: Love *h*eals.
Old belief: Men don't love me the way I want.	New belief: Men are emotionally available to me.

Notice the word count does not have to be exact. However, it must be very close to match the syntax.

Now you know how to ***Recognize*** what you want to change. You know how to compare the belief you have determined needs changing, within your life experience. You know how to word a new belief so that it will "fit" into your subconscious mind.

Step one is complete. The process of permanent change is in play. The primary question, as we take the second step, continues to be are we willing to change? Not an easy question. Adam and I both had to choose if we were willing to explore ourselves, at the depth it would take to create permanent change. We knew our relationship would not survive without that change, but isn't love worth the risk?

CHAPTER ELEVEN:

Acknowledge

SINCE BEFORE the written word, songwriters have proclaimed that it is love that matters, it is love that molds our life's journey. Love was certainly the reason both Adam and I were willing to risk the uncertainty of our love story. It was the reason we were willing to peel away the parts of ourselves that resisted love - even destroyed it.

Love is a risk most of us say we are willing to take, yet too few of us really do. It demands total honesty to ourselves and to the one we love, regardless of the impact to ourselves. Love demands honesty.

> Remember Adam's words to me,
> *"I sense that you feel me slipping from you, and us, as you show me a path to my fantasy…I will hold the space for you…and for us. I know you to be courageous and brave…as from a place of integrity you speak to my higher good, at potential cost to yourself…"*

As together, you and I, move into step two of the Change Process, hold on tightly to the parts of you that want a healthy love. Hold on tight to the parts of you that want to create the love of your life. Let those parts of you move you forward into the unknown.

> **Secret:** ***In order to create love you must understand why you do not want it.***

Telling ourselves the truth about why we have clung to a belief that has repeatedly caused us harm, takes courage. It is a step that must be done with rigorous honesty and compassionate gentleness to ourselves. Self-discovery demands both.

Step 2: Acknowledge

Acknowledging is a two-phase process:

1. We gain an understanding of why we created and maintained a belief that does not work for us.
2. We accept responsibility for the *impact* this feeling has on ourselves, and others.

The first phase of acknowledging involves discovering the hidden motives behind the belief you have held onto for so long. You can find those hidden motives by learning about your emotional payoffs.

Understanding

At one time or another, each of us has realized that we persist in feelings or behaviors that are destructive to us. We know it and we see it clearly. We even promise ourselves to change, yet we continue to repeat the same pattern. Why?

The answers to this question are varied and intricate. You and I continue these patterns that do not work for us because we receive some kind of benefit, some emotional payoff, for our feelings or behavior. Discovering our payoffs is a vital step toward understanding why we cling to our past, and our old beliefs. It is also an important step toward accepting responsibility for the impact that maintaining the old belief has had on ourselves, and others.

When Adam realized that he created his own reality he bravely turned inside of himself to discover more. One of the many aspects of Adam that I love is his willingness to use what he learns. In this case, he was seeking to understand what parts of him were hanging onto his old beliefs. He was seeking to understand his "payoffs" for holding so tenaciously to the past.

Adam, you and I have repeatedly clung to the past. We have defended our behavior and our beliefs. Has it worked for you? Do you have the love life you want? Do you have the life you want?

If you are ready, why don't we continue our journey and find out what we gained by holding onto destructive beliefs? We can then consciously choose to let the old beliefs go.

24 Days, 0 Hrs, 45 Mins

SUBJECT: ***Love***

Hello beautiful :-)

Thank you (dhanaybath…pronounced 'dunn-ya-butt') lol…for your beautiful and supportive missive…I feel very loved! No really! I do! Thank you also for removing any obstacle to my growth and demonstrating that true love really has nothing to do with control, agendas, or loss! It got me thinking about my first paradigm take on true love. My higher self, timely as always, prodded me and I recalled these lyrics from my favorite band.

"Love; it will not betray you, dismay or enslave you, it will set you free, be more like the man you were made to be." Mumford

and Sons (from the song "Sigh no more"—2009)

I've sung these lyrics many times…but it's not until I truly paid attention that I finally understood…and when I did…I cried… literally…in a café…not sobs…just tears. Hopeless!

As you can appreciate…I'm going through a process and I imagine I will for some time yet…you have a head start …

First, I'm identifying and defining my current paradigm (the first one) and once I have owned up to it and explored every bit of beauty and ugliness, I will move on to one I want to create (the second paradigm)…just like you are…I love your analogy and metaphors…in a sense you are trailblazing for me…a swashbuckling buccaneer! The explorer in me is already there…and he is tapping his foot, wondering why he is the only one there (on your metaphorical shore :-) I am calling to him from the ship telling him there is still much work to do on the ship!

I'm getting ready for my personal exposition…tackling the Questions…I know this is going to be "full on" and raw…so I just have to keep going…one step at a time! I can see you :-) but I'm still frightened…:-/

xoxoxoxoxo

Adam

Payoff Questions[4]

Payoff questions help us identify what we get by maintaining our old beliefs.

We are not stupid, yet we cling to old beliefs that hurt us. There has to be a reason for that. The reason is quite simply because we get something from that old belief, something so important that we risk the pain of the old belief. By identifying what that payoff is we can consciously choose to let go.

The following questions helped me discover exactly what my payoffs were for hanging on to my old belief, "Men don't love me the way I want to be loved." Adam had to dig in and confront his reasons for hanging onto the belief, "Women betray."

These payoff questions allowed both of us to take a deeper look. They can be used for *any* behavior, thought, feeling, or belief you would like to change. The goal of these questions is to awaken our consciousness to the motives behind keeping them. When you answer these questions honestly, you can eliminate the possibility of using your subconscious mind as an excuse for feelings and behaviors that hurt you, or others.

Since it will be important to use these questions on a regular basis, each question is assigned a key word for easy recall.

Key Word: Avoid

What am I trying to avoid by maintaining my current belief?

This question can be answered by exploring what feelings we are trying *not* to feel, and what actions we try *not* to make. When we think of the word *avoid*, we usually think of emotions we label negative, such as hurt, hate, anger, and jealousy. Yet, we often try to avoid positive feelings such as success, love, and responsibility as well. Any time our beliefs eliminate any form of goodness from our lives, we are actually avoiding the full spectrum of our feelings. For example, if we consistently fail in our relationships, perhaps we want to avoid the positive feelings of intimacy, love, and happiness.

Look at this question deeply. When we do we will almost always discover both positive and constricting emotions that we are avoiding. For example, if I had clung to the belief that "Men will never love me the way I want to be loved," then no matter what Adam did I would feel unloved in some capacity. By clinging to this old belief I would have been avoiding facing the feelings of being "too much for a man" and simultaneously, "not being enough" to warrant a man's love.

You might rightfully say, "Stop, that does not make sense. Your belief keeps you from love, assuring that Adam cannot love you the way you want. Why would you cling to that?" Good point, why would I? Why would any of us cling to beliefs that hurt us so badly?

If my pattern, because of my belief, is to create men who fail to love me the way I want, then I never have to risk total immersion into love. I do not have to risk losing the "real thing." I will get hurt, no doubt. But I will not be destroyed, as I feared I would if I lost the love of my life after he and I had totally committed. When we avoid something wonderful, we are doing so because we fear the loss of that and we are running from the pain of that loss.

Now let's keep walking the rocky path of self-discovery. What else was I avoiding by creating men who did not love me the way I wanted to be loved? What else was I avoiding? True intimacy! Now that is really frightening. Intimacy, by definition, demands closeness, openness, tenderness, vulnerability, trust, caring, and knowing. If any of these is too frightening to risk, if they demand too much courage, then it is not the fear of being unloved I am running from; no, it is the risk of intimacy.

These questions on the surface are deceptively simplistic. They are not. They are avenues of self-exploration that can uncover our real agendas for hanging onto beliefs that hurt us so terribly.

Key Word: Righteousness

What righteous feelings am I hanging onto?

This question helps us explore feelings we think we have earned the right to feel. We often use these righteous feelings as a shield, to protect us from further hurt. The trouble is, it doesn't work. For example, someone has hurt us and therefore we have a right to be angry. This question asks us to explore feelings we cling to, feelings we have justified because of our past experiences.

For instance, Adam was badly betrayed by a series of women. I bet you can guess who was the first woman who betrayed him. You bet, his mother. He had a long list of excellent "reasons" to feel righteous anger. Now, Adam is a sophisticated and intelligent man. He would never come right out and say, or even think, that all women betray. But he behaves as if they will. He has a belief that they will and consequently, in his perception, all women betray him. He, by virtue of this belief, had to see my lying by omission about my age as a betrayal. He then, in turn, had the "right" to be angry, even raging, at that betrayal.

Any time we add righteousness to a feeling, we eliminate the possibility of releasing the feeling because righteousness is like superglue. It keeps us stuck in a feeling for as long as we hold onto our righteousness. Adam might reasonably say, "I have the *right* to feel as I do!" Yes, he does. He has the right and that "right" will destroy any hope he has of lasting love until he released the "right" so the feelings of rage can be felt and released.

When considering the belief you want to change, what feeling are you refusing to release?

Key Word: Blame

Who am I trying to blame—either out of misguided love, or the desire to punish—for my current behavior?

To make it easier, ask yourself, "Who am I loving or who am I punishing by clinging to my old belief?" Many times, we continue unhealthy behavior and hold destructive beliefs, because we are trying to punish or show love for another. We may not notice we are actually blaming those we want to punish—or love—for our circumstances. In your search for the answer to this question, always look to the ones that parented you regardless of their title: mother, father, aunt, uncle, grandmother, grandfather, foster mother or stepfather.

Let's continue with the example of Adam's belief, "Women betray." Why was he clinging to this belief? What was the payoff? When we answer the question for ourselves, we will need to look at both sides of the question. For example, Adam, as a way to show love for his mother, may continue to create women who, in one respect or another, betray him. The child-self clings and says, "See Mom? I love you so much I create women just like you."

OR, Adam's way of punishing his mother could be saying, "You are the reason I cannot really trust women. Look at me. Look at my life. You are the reason I have suffered so much. You are to blame for all my pain."

A quick aside: Each of us has a child-self and adolescent-self within us. You have heard that many times. What you might not know is that a child will sacrifice itself in order to be loved by their mother and/or father. If that wounded child is still living within you, and has not been healed, it will sacrifice your adult life trying to get the love they did not get as a child.

Blame, motivated by old beliefs, can destroy our quest for almost anything—certainly love. Answering the question of who we are trying to blame, through misguided love or the desire to punish, will help us unveil our camouflaged excuses for not creating what we say we want—love. At first, the answers might not be obvious. However, our behavior can give us insight into motivations that are deeper than we usually look. In this case we are looking for the people we blame for the lack of love in our lives.

Key Word: Guarantee

What guarantee do I want from God before I will be willing to change my beliefs?

A guarantee might sound something like this, "Before I agree to be really vulnerable in this relationship, I want God to promise I'll never be hurt," or, "Before I really put all of my heart into this relationship, I must know s/he is the 'one'." Since guarantees illuminate our secret fears, this question helps us discover them. In the first example, by demanding a guarantee that we will not be hurt, we expose our fear/belief that we will. In the second example, our fear of discovering, after we gave our heart, that s/he is not the one who will love us forever, reveals our fear of losing love or of not being enough for that love. Consequently, we demand the guarantee from God.

Before you risk love, what must God promise you will happen or will not happen?

Key Word: Self-Pity

How much pleasure do I get from self-pity?

For many, self-pity is obvious. We walk around complaining about the quality of our life. We believe we are victims of bad luck, unfortunate circumstances, loser men or betraying women. For some of us, this hangdog kind of self-pity is overt. However, most of us prefer to be much more subtle. Yet the very nature of our subtlety deludes us into believing we are not indulging in self-pity.

Before skipping this payoff question as not applicable to you, take a second look. Self-pity also manifests as frustration or anger at things that never go quite right. For example, maybe you attract women who pretend to like you just the way you are, including your sports Sundays. Then you discover she hates sports. You get angry and frustrated and say, "Women cannot be trusted to tell you the truth, they just wait for you to be in love and then they pounce and start changing you." That is self-pity. Or perhaps you say to your girlfriends, "There are just no adult men out there. They are all little boys." That is self-pity.

How does your self-pity manifest itself?

Key Word: Self-Importance

How does my behavior make me feel better than other people?

Does this sound like the voice in your head? "My case is special. I have suffered for so long, that I could not possibly use this information or do the exercises. They will not work for me. I need special attention and special exercises just for me." This I-have-it-so-bad scenario is only one side of the self-importance coin. Notice how being "the worst" at something can make us feel as arrogant as being "the best." In this case, the person is the best at being the worst.

Self-importance can also sound like this: "Listen, I'm not as crippled as the women/men I see around me. I have my act together. There is really nothing anyone can tell me about my life that I do not already know." In this case the person has nothing to learn and no self-discovery to be made, because they already know it all. Another aspect of this side of the coin involves feelings of importance, based on circumstances of birth, geographic location, or financial status.

What is true for you? Are you the "best" worst or the "best" of the best?

Key Word: The Past

Why am I clinging to the past?

Some of us hold on to our old beliefs simply because we are not willing to do the work required to move ahead. Others are afraid to move out of the past because we lack the skills required to handle life situations in new and different ways.

Still others have no intention of even considering change because, somewhere within us, we know that if we change we will have to give up manipulation, domination, and self-centered behavior. Finally, many of us remain stuck in the past because we fear the unknown, not knowing if we will be able to cope with the future.

What is true for you? Why have you clung to a past perpetrated by your old beliefs? What is so important about the past that you will not risk a different future?

Adam and I had to wade our way through these payoffs. By understanding how the old beliefs served us, we could begin to let go. As we understood how we were trying to protect ourselves from pain and hurt, we could be compassionate with ourselves. We shook our heads at how long we had suffered, simply because we did not have the tools to understand the "why" of our behaviors. Once we did, letting them go was a conscious choice.

Are you ready? The outcome of really digging in and looking at "why" can be compassion, insight, wry humor, and a willingness to let go and change.

Homegrowth 4: Exploring the Why

1. Write down the belief you have decided to change and answer all of the Payoff Questions.
2. You will find it more beneficial to write these questions in the form of self-dialogue rather than as short-sentence or one-word answers. Or record your answers and then listen to what you had to say.
3. Avoid: What am I trying to avoid by maintaining my current belief?
4. Righteousness: What righteous feelings am I hanging onto?
5. Blame: Who am I trying to blame—either out of misguided love or the desire to punish—for my current behavior?

6. Guarantee: What guarantee do I want before I will be willing to change?
7. Self-pity: How much pleasure do I get from self-pity?
8. Self-importance: How does my belief and subsequent behavior make me better than other people?
9. The Past: Why am I clinging to the past?

As you get familiar with your payoffs and how they work, you will discover you have two or three payoffs you use most frequently. Maybe you blame as a knee-jerk reaction. Maybe you will not move an inch until God promises you that you will not be hurt again. Maybe everyone you know has heard your story of woe, and you are lost in self-pity. As you become familiar with your payoffs, you will be able to identify your unique pattern.

Recognizing our payoffs leads to a deeper understanding of our beliefs, feelings, and behavior. These new understandings allow us to take responsibility for our *impact* on ourselves, and others. Our constricting beliefs, the ones that cause us repeated harm, also harm those whom we love and who love us. Before we can take responsibility for our impact, let's investigate what impact is.

CHAPTER TWELVE:

Impact

Impact is the effect our beliefs, feelings, and behaviors have on the world around us. Because we have an innate desire to bond, we have agreed to have impact on others, and to be impacted by them. Creating the love of your life without allowing impact would be impossible.

Adam and I risked that impact. We could only be responsible for ourselves, and risking love meant the other could have an impact that hurt. Adam came out of his man-cave and wrote:

24 Days, 9 Hrs, 20 Mins

SUBJECT: ***Hi Beautiful***

Hi beautiful :-)

It's me!

I just realized that I have now been in Nepal for nine days and my body clock has only now just reset itself…not helped by a woman screaming for her partner to get out of their room (only a few doors down from mine) at midnight. That made me think about what agendas and subtexts are running in that relationship...the controls and fears and lack in each...it also took me back to my experiences as a policeman of the many, many situations of domestic violence that have since blurred into one amalgam of pain and fear...of grasping and clinging...at the unconscious mass of people who don't know the meaning of true love, of being happy in the self.

If anything, it has further steeled my resolve to continue this journey into my heart. I have been on this journey since April of this year, when the first references to true love appear in my journal.

My beautiful connection with you has given me structure and shone a light on the way ahead, the beginning of the trail, your gentle hand on me, soothing my fears, your beautiful feminine heart whispering encouragement...and whilst I know that we are on the same path...I am unable to be with you now.

You have already journeyed through the "switchbacks," bramble bushes, bogs and marshes, braved freezing nights, and are now sitting atop a sunlit ridge with a smile on your face, and beauty in your heart...I know I am capable, deserving of the same love you are experiencing...and even though the distance is great, I am committed. I will ascend the ridge too...or journey to the center of the labyrinth, or do my housekeeping on the ship and journey to the shore...to your grotto...to be kissed by the goddess :-)

I know we are not a "couple" as you mention, and I'm mourning this. I know that I cannot commit to us or to you. You are everything I asked the universe for...everything! And true to her word the Goddess gave...I am very grateful. Our relationship (and the Universe already knew) highlighted areas for me to grow, to learn…my life's purpose is here…and clarity beckons.

I'm embarking on an introspective journey. This is my choice. I am not mired in the first paradigm by any measure, but must understand my origins, before I move on. I will join you in the second paradigm, but I do not know when or in what capacity.

I have a lump in my heart. I think this is sorrow. I'm going to mourn us, the possibility of us…all the while acknowledging the grace and beauty of what we have…what you mean to me and that you are in my heart forever.

I know you understand the "why" of this.

I know you said you would feel humiliated…because you have shown too much of yourself and made yourself completely vulnerable. I don't want you to feel like this…I have laid myself bare, as you have. I have been introduced to the most extraordinary woman I have ever met…and I'm freely letting her go. How does this make sense? It's because of the example you have shown me…the love…freely given, as you quest for your heart. It's my heart's journey too…so you will know that I am honored to have shared your space.

I know you will be upset, but I will continue to write to you until you tell me to stop. I want to share my journey with you, not because I need guidance or to be taught, or there is a lack somewhere but because I am so close to you, and I want to share my experience, discovery, and joy with you. You don't have to respond, I seek nothing in return, only that I be permitted to write my thoughts so you can know my journey.

You are a beautiful woman :-)

xoxoxo

Adam

In between the lovely words was goodbye. To say that it had impact is a monumental understatement. In my heart, I had continued to hope. Adam's missives in those last few days had felt like one step forward into hope, two steps back into old beliefs and fears.

I knew Adam did not have the tools yet to change his beliefs. I wish he had waited until he had, but he chose to end our relationship without waiting to develop those tools. In my pain and hurt, my one goal was to take responsibility for creating a man of great brilliance and love who was stuck in his past and fighting his way out of it. I also had to take responsibility to stay in the new paradigm of vulnerability and humility. I had to resist the old habits of blame, manipulation, or hurting him in return. I had to look at why I did not want his love, because after all it was the reality I was creating.

25 Days, 8 Hrs, 54 Mins

So I replied:

SUBJECT: ***Mourning***

> *Oh Adam…yes it hurts and I mourn my loss of you. Mourning doesn't seem to be a big enough word.*
>
> *Yes, I understand, and yes, I want what is best for you. Have a glorious journey into more of yourself.*
>
> *In my heart of hearts I hoped you would find your way to us some day. I think you just told me there is no possibility of that, and to have one would be to hinder you. I think you just set me free and told me not to wait for you, not to hope. This separation from your love hurts. I know you are not saying you don't care for or about me, rather you are saying you must first care about yourself. I can do nothing but agree and mourn.*

Yes write, and if it is too painful for me I will let you know. I do love you so and will step back now, as I believe this missive has asked me to do? If I am wrong about what you have said, or what is in your heart, let me know.

Dear Adam, Goddess knows I will miss you in my heart beyond measure. I will send love and energy to your higher self so he may use it in any way that is for your highest good.

I just can't get myself to write the word goodbye, so instead I will say fare well my dear love.

K

Self-honoring beliefs, feelings, and behaviors are not truly harmful to others. However, impact caused by old constricting beliefs, feelings, and behaviors can and do damage to us, and those we care about.

While it was key to my life that I felt deeply, and moved into, and through my feeling about Adam's decision, what good would it do me to rail at Adam? I knew he was acting on old beliefs. His decision was that he was not ready, nor willing to risk the kind of love we had set out to create together. He believed that it wasn't me he was meant to love. Adam wrestled with his mind and heart, forgetting, or perhaps not really understanding, that both are programmed by his beliefs. Adam loved and honored himself by wrestling with the lesser parts of him. In his missive he was speaking his truth, as he knew it. I could do nothing but honor his decisions, regardless of whether I agreed or not.

It is important to consider both ourselves and those we care about, when examining our negative impact. As I have mentioned, most of us have never learned to love ourselves. We never learned to honor ourselves as the most precious beings in our lives. Hence, we continue in self-destructive behaviors, wallowing in self-pity and believing we are never good enough. We alone are responsible for this negative impact on our lives. When we take responsibility for that impact, we take one more step toward changing those old beliefs.

If you take the time to go back and reread some of Adam's missives to me, you will see his doubt about being enough for me. You now have the skills to begin to recognize his beliefs. Remember one of the Secrets: *we only need to examine what we have in our own lives to know what we believe*.

Keep in mind that Adam wrote just a few days earlier, "I am standing at the entrance to the labyrinth…and I see you…I want to come to you, but I have such a long way to go…*are you sure you want me to come?*" And in the same missive, "I'm scared to love you…I will be opened like never before…I want to work on myself…and I'm scared."

You can recognize the beliefs he must hold about himself to continually ask me how I knew I loved him, and his concern about not being enough for me. Adam was not bad or wrong. No, he was immensely courageous to look at himself with the tools that he had. Adam was "miswired," he had beliefs that did not work for him when it comes to love and women.

I also had bad wiring; I had beliefs that did not work for me. With the help of both my mentors, I changed those beliefs.

Standing in the first paradigm of love—one that wants another to fulfill lacks, there are agendas that weaken love, and beliefs that cannot sustain love, and almost always this means love will die. Sadly, Adam and I began with both of us standing in this first paradigm of love.

Perhaps the more important aspect of impact is accepting responsibility for the negative impact we have on those we care about. Accepting this responsibility is the clearest way to perceive the power of impact. Sometimes, realizing just how destructive we are to those we love, can motivate us to do the work necessary to change.

When we take responsibility for the negative impact we have on those around us, we focus on the emotional damage we cause.

We seek out and discover our "uglies"—the hurt-filled fears, manipulations, dominations and controls that are part of our daily lives. For some of us, seeing our negative impact will be obvious. Others of us, whose "uglies" are camouflaged in subtle maneuverings, will have to search more diligently.

Homegrowth 5: Impact and Responsibility

Every single one of us has hurt someone because of our constricting beliefs and subsequent attitudes, thoughts, feelings, decisions, and choices. Evaluating how we have hurt others can give us continued motivation on our journey of permanent change. Let's take an example of how negative beliefs first affect ourselves, and then take it further, and examine how that same negative belief also affects those around us.

EXAMPLE:

Avoid (impact on myself):

- By avoiding relationships, I am depriving myself of love and intimacy. I am unhappy.

Righteous (impact on myself)

- By having the right to be angry, I create other angry people around me and that is painful.

EXAMPLE:

Avoid (impact on others):

- Because I am unhappy, I am often short-tempered, especially at the opposite sex whom I blame for my unhappiness.

Righteous (impact on others):

- I use my anger and righteousness to lash out and suppress others, or perhaps more subtly, punishing them by withholding, being sarcastic or insultingly superior.

Write about the impact each payoff has had on the people you care about in your life. You will want to take the time to think about your impact and write out all your feelings in detail. Ask yourself:

1. What was my hurtful behavior?
2. How did my behavior affect the other person?
3. Why did I want to hurt him or her? (We never accidently hurt someone else. There is always a motive somewhere, no matter how carefully buried.)

Payoff Antidotes[5]

Now that we know our payoffs and have accepted responsibility for their impact, we have the power to do something about them. In order to defuse the payoffs, we can learn to alter our responses to them. By choosing a response that will counteract the effects of our self-destructive behavior, we can detoxify our payoffs.

Each payoff has an antidote that can help us move out of unhealthy feelings and behaviors. The key words for the antidotes are identical to those of the payoffs.

Antidote for *Avoid*: Tell yourself the truth.

By honestly facing the issues we previously sidestepped, we can detoxify this payoff. For instance, if I have discovered I am avoiding the happiness inherent in self-love, then I need to consider why I fear happiness. If I can tell myself the truth, "I'm afraid of happiness," I can then deal with the fear and move on.

Antidote for *Righteousness*: Let go of the hurt and anger.

Since most of our righteousness centers around feelings of hurt and anger, we can learn to release these feelings. We can do the work it takes to heal the hurt, often by getting help. We can learn to express our anger in a healthy way, and by so doing, release it. When we decide not to punish others, we can release the protective shield of righteousness.

Antidote for *Blame*

1. Process your feelings.
2. Accept responsibility.

By acknowledging and processing the feelings that produced the blame, we begin to clear blame. Then, as we take responsibility, by discovering what belief(s) caused the situation, we can defuse blame's toxicity.

Antidote for *Guarantee*: Accept total responsibility.

Accepting responsibility for absolutely everything we create is the antidote for needing a guarantee before we will take risks. By taking total responsibility for creating our lives, we can evaluate our choices more consciously. When we know we are responsible for everything that happens in our lives, it is easier to make decisions and choices that honor us. When we take responsibility, it is easier to love ourselves. When we make choices that honor us, we no longer need a guarantee from the God. Our self-love and self-honoring choices are our guarantee.

Antidote for *Self-Importance*: Develop self-intimacy.

Since self-importance stems from feelings of inadequacy, the antidote is to become intimate with ourselves. Spend time getting to know yourself; learn to recognize your value. Working through this book is an excellent step in the pursuit of self-intimacy.

Antidote for Self-Pity: Ask for and receive help.
To end self-pity, sincerely ask for help and utilize it when it is extended. It is impossible to feel sorry for ourselves when we are asking for and receiving help.

Antidote for *the Past*: Let go of old patterns.
The way to let go of the past is to explore, identify, and change old feelings and patterns that no longer serve us. It is also important to stay current with our present feelings.

Congratulations, we are now halfway through the Change Process. As you get better at discerning and telling yourself the truth, the first two steps can be completed with total impeccability in under an hour.

1. Recognize (what beliefs you want to change)
2. Acknowledge (what you received by hanging on to the belief)
    a. *Understand* why you believe, feel, and behave as you do by learning about your payoffs.
    b. *Accept* responsibility for your *impact* on yourself and others.

Adam did not give himself the chance to walk this process, step by step, before he decided I was not the woman he could love. Was the fear too great? Was the risk not worth it to him? Had he never intended for our affair to turn into love? Was I not the right woman for him and he just did not love me? Whatever the reason, he had made his choice.

I had given myself the opportunity to change my beliefs, indeed to change paradigms. In all fairness, we need to remember I have been changing my beliefs for decades. I have taught this topic all over the world. I, as Adam so rightly put it, had "a head start."

Yet, we both jumped in heart first. We were intrepid seekers of love and wanted to explore what we could create together. In doing so we were both responsible for our impact on ourselves and one another. We are ultimately responsible for what we allowed and did not allow. Each of us will have to forgive ourselves for our impact on ourselves, and on each other. Forgiveness is the linchpin in change, and is the next step in the Change Process.

CHAPTER THIRTEEN:

Forgive

WHEN YOU AND I want to create a new reality, when we want to permanently transform our love life, as was promised in the title of this book, we must be willing to forgive. Forgiveness begins with being absolutely clear as to "what." What happened that caused us harm? What do we need to forgive? And perhaps surprisingly, "who" do we need to forgive? As we continue this journey together, keep this thought in the front of your mind; we create our own experience, our own reality, all of it!

Step 3: Forgive

27 Days, 3 Hrs, 59 Mins

SUBJECT: ***It's Me***

Dearest Kimberley,

Please don't say goodbye—you are in my heart now. I deeply care for you and about you…more than you know. I know it must have been difficult to wake to read my last missive…I really felt you in this moment. I spent hours crafting it…to read the way you would understand it, and what I actually meant to say…I hope you don't think poorly of me for writing, rather than waiting to see you again.

I thought more about your love for me and how you knew…like, really knew that you loved me…I deduced that you knew because your heart told you so. It was a feeling you had…the certainty you felt is what has eluded me. My head made up excuses, sure…and you know about those. But when I swept those silly negative ego issues aside and got deep into my heart…searching for my knowing, I had to admit that, even though I wanted so much to follow you to the center of the labyrinth and declare my love for you and commit my heart with yours…I could not.

I had attracted into my life the most beautiful and extraordinary woman I have ever met. There she was…my dearest Kimberley, wanting me and loving me…your desire was so attractive. So, why couldn't I commit to her and confess my love? And what role does my heart play in all of this?

I had attracted you because you are what I asked the Goddess for…my perfect spiritual woman, with love, integrity, grace and honor…in all your beauty. However, I had figured out that, as you listened to your heart to find answers, so must I. In my man-cave, I had a raging battle between my heart and my head…and in the end, I knew I would be perpetrating a fraud on both of us, if I committed my half-hearted heart to you. My heart heaves with sorrow as my truth became a knowing…I hope you do not feel misled by me.

Full Stop

There was something about Adam's words, "I hope you do not feel misled by me," that outraged me. After all, from the beginning he proclaimed I was a gift from the Goddess and then, after opening the gift, admiring its shiny content and playing with it for a while, he gave it, "me"…back.

You might ask, "Didn't you feel hurt, anger, rage, frustration, and pain?" The answer is, of course I did! In that moment I felt all of those things—all at once. When I could slow down my breathing and give myself a moment, I began to discern what emotions I was feeling. I realized that what I felt was more anger than rage, more outrage than rage, more hurt than pain, and I was certainly frustrated.

When I read those words again, "I hope you do not feel misled by me," I wanted to punch him. If he had been in the same room with me, I would have had to leave because I wanted to hurt him. Not very spiritual I know, but there it was. In that moment, I was out of compassion for Adam and his struggles with his emotions. In that moment I could only feel my own hurt and anger.

When I could function again, I did the only thing I could do to stay solidly in the new paradigm, and that was to look inside myself for answers. It was up to me to heal myself, getting any help I needed, and then I could move ahead.

So, I set to work immediately. I did not wait for the feelings to fester and grow. Instead I walked into them. I felt the anger and outrage in the safe confines of my home. I cried when the anger was spent and the hurt surfaced. The anger came in waves, just when I thought I was through it another wave smacked me. I used the techniques I had learned over many years of self-growth, as again and again the anger hit, resolved, and hurt emerged. I vented my outrage in a missive to Adam that I knew, even as I wrote it, that I would never send. I wanted to dump the poison on paper, not carry it with me or dump it on him. Finally, spent, I sat on my couch and looked out at the sea. In the stillness I centered and gave myself the gift of healing.

I continued to expose my feelings to myself when they surfaced. The more I worked, the more the nuances of unresolved feelings surfaced to be resolved. Each time, I experienced more intense feelings and explored the "why" of what I had created with Adam. The process of discovering, feeling, and letting go continued.

In short, I did exactly what we have been doing in the Change Process. This time, not changing a belief, but rather changing what could have been the negative long-term impact of Adam's choice not to love me or continue in the journey of "us."

First, I ***Recognized*** the parts of me that were hurting. I went to work in meditation. I filled the lack in my child-self (desire for Adam to love her), and gave her what she really needed, my love. My adolescent-self was stunned, and wanted to withdraw from life and sulk. She wanted to drag out the healing, as if that would prove to the world how deeply she loved. I let her be melodramatic in her world, not mine. Again, in meditation, I helped her create a boy who she thought was cute, one who returned her affections. Adam was quickly forgotten.

With my child-self and adolescent-self no longer affecting my perceptions, I, the adult woman, could move to the next step. I ***Acknowledged*** my feelings and felt them again and again until the energy behind them was spent.

Solidly planted in the new paradigm of vulnerability, humility, and intimacy, I could love completely, and just as completely, mourn the loss. I did not need to suffer endlessly to prove my love for Adam to myself, or for that matter, to anyone else. When new feelings surfaced, as they did, I worked my way through them, rather than deny them. I did not hug them to my heart as a red badge of courage, or as proof of my love.

Secret: ***Suffering for long periods of time does not mean your love is any deeper, or more profound, than if you had healed yourself in the first days or weeks of your loss. (Remember, get help, as much help as you need to resolve your hurt as soon as you can.)***

The rest of Adam's missive, the one that finally made clear to me he was not going to allow us the opportunity to journey any further together, went like this:

In a very short month, I have learned so much about myself and about you. I have a greater understanding of my path. I know these words will be difficult to read...almost as difficult as they are writing them. But I wish to honor you, and your integrity, with my truth, so that you will know that you are always with me, in my being.

I was thinking (if it hasn't already been done yet) you could call your next book "The Second Paradigm" and you could explore the link between the heart and the illusory world as we know it, then by contrast, offer the insight of the second paradigm...of true love, how you (and I) are experiencing it ...

Apart from a study in catharsis i.e., moving from the first to the second paradigm, such a study would bring the planet closer to understanding what it is we are actually all doing here...anyway...but just a thought ...

Anyway, gorgeous...I will write again.

Please take care of you xoxoxox

Adam :-)

Adam had already moved on. He was done with "us" and even encouraged me to write this book. I knew I was not done. If I never wanted this to happen again, I had to complete the Change Process. I knew I had to forgive. Forgive the "who" for "what they did" became the journey.

I know you are going to be yelling at me at this point, "Screw that! Don't forgive the jerk. He led you on, then dumped you." But you see, that would be the wrong solution for me. Adam longed for what he would not risk. He had created his fantasy woman, and when fantasy became reality, he ran. He was never a jerk, just limited in what he was willing to brave in the name of love.

As far as dumping me, well, yes, he did. He told himself he had to, in order to honor what was true for him. He was not cavalier, nor malicious. With all that said, I did not have to like or agree with his decisions. I had fought for "us" as long and as hard as I was willing. Now, I had to accept what was true: Adam did not want to love me.

Full circle, I created my own reality through my belief, colored by my attitudes, thoughts, feelings, decisions, and ultimately my choices. Adam was my choice. I wanted to jump in with him, heart first. I thought he was everything I wanted. Relationships are a journey of discovery: sometimes you are just wrong.

Without diminishing Adam, I was wrong about him and us. He was unwilling to step into the world in which I was now living. So "what" and "who" do I need to forgive?

The first step in forgiving is understanding what forgiveness is, and what it is not. There are three basic types of forgiveness. First, there is universal forgiveness, which entails asking to be forgiven by the Divine by whatever name. Second, there is forgiveness for and from other human beings. Last—and critically—there is self-forgiveness. You and I are going to explore self-forgiveness, and forgiving another.

Secret: ***In forgiveness always start with yourself.***

Self-Forgiveness

I would tell you that forgiveness is almost like magic, but that would diminish the power of forgiveness. Forgiveness is not *almost* like magic, it is flat out magical. Forgiveness, with all of its energy and grace, sets up a chain reaction within us that can change our lives. The mystery of forgiveness is that we don't know "how" it works, we just understand that it does. Forgiveness leads to new levels of expectation. These new levels of expectation lead to deeper and more vivid imagination. Imagination, the most powerful tool of creation, leads to allowing miracles. And miracles lead to transcendent moments. We do not know exactly how forgiveness works, but we can experience the chain reaction: the healing and the magic that it brings to us.

Forgiveness is the third critical step in the Change Process. If I could not forgive myself for creating a man, Adam, who was not willing to brave the fear of intimacy and love at the depth in which I want to live, then I would be a "victim" of our short-lived relationship.

It was I who needed to forgive myself for my own limitations. If I would forgive myself for once more creating someone who reflected back to me my own beliefs of "being too much, too intense" and for my love "not being enough," then I could heal. Self-forgiveness could lift me to greater expectations for my life. I could imagine a relationship that did have all I want. I could allow gifts from the Divine, which we call miracles, and I could, in that moment, be changed—a transcendent moment. Self-forgiveness needed to come before forgiving Adam. Adam did not create my life; he had impact upon it. I am the creator of my life, as we have spoken about repeatedly, so it follows that I must forgive myself first.

Sometimes we forgive ourselves for past behaviors for which we are not proud. For instance, I had to forgive myself for lying to Adam by omission; not sharing my age. However, in this third step of the Change Process I had to forgive myself for a miswired belief. I began a relationship from the foundation of "lack." Why did I lie to Adam? Because I felt lacking, as if there was something wrong with being older than him. I went into the relationship wanting him to love me in ways I was not willing to love myself. I created our relationship from lack, and that foundation helped destroyed us.

What this means is that I needed to heal, and forgive various aspects of myself that believed in the "lack." We give these aspects names to make them easier to imagine and work with, such as: child-self, adolescent, me-the-lesser, and negative ego. These parts of me tenaciously held on to beliefs that no longer protected or honored me.

We need to forgive the aspects of ourselves that have worked against us. When we forgive these aspects of ourselves that have worked against us, we receive a greater gift of self-understanding. We forgive the "why," as I outlined in step two of the Change Process.

Remember, the steps of change don't change: Recognize, Acknowledge, Forgive, and Change. Forgiveness initiates miracles in our reality, and in the world. Forgive and then integrate the part of yourself that you have forgiven.

> **Secret:** ***It's important to know that after forgiving, you will have learned something more about yourself. In that moment of forgiving you might not know what has been unveiled to you...give it time, and you will come to know.***

> **Secret:** ***When you forgive yourself, let that part of you come back to you, and be part of the whole again.***

Self-forgiveness is the ability to let go of the feelings of self-condemnation and self-anger. Self-forgiveness is a powerful act of loving kindness. When we forgive ourselves, we let go of the self-condemning parts of us and allow ourselves the freedom to embrace a more loving future.

Homegrowth 6: Self-Forgiveness Finally Free

1. Review the work you completed in *Homegrowth 5: Impact and Responsibility*, page 171.
2. Write out on a sheet of paper, "What do I *think*? What part of me do I want to forgive?" (The child self, the lonely self, the arrogant self, etc. Do not get lost in the labels.)
3. What do I *feel*? What feelings are coming up? There will be an array of feelings, not just one.
4. What did I learn about myself? Look at your life; what happened? What did the part of you that caused your current hurt do, that needs to forgive? (Did you abandon yourself? Did you give your power away? Did you consciously hurt another? Did you want someone else to be responsible for your happiness?)
5. Feel the remorse: "I'm human, I make mistakes." This is about feeling really sorry for what you have done. It is not about feeling sorry for yourself.
6. Forgive yourself by completing the *Forgiveness Meditation*, page 219. This meditation should leave you feeling lighter, freer, and more at peace. It is geared to communicate with both your conscious and subconscious minds, thus allowing self-forgiveness to be more complete.
7. Repeat this meditation until your heart and your gut tell you that you have truly forgiven yourself.
8. Even if you do none of the other exercises in this book, this one *Homegrowth* exercise can change your life. This is the power of self-forgiveness.
9. "What do I do, or what don't I do NOW?" Start with what you don't have to do anymore. Example: "I don't have to be afraid anymore. I can reveal the real me."
10. "What do I *feel* now?"
11. "What do I *think* now?"

Forgiving Another

Repeat the process, but this time answer the questions with the other person in mind. Discover "why" they did what they did and forgive that, just as you forgave yourself.

From this new plateau—that one can only stand upon after we have forgiven, you and I can perceive the world differently. We will experience our lives and the people in it differently. This is the power of self-forgiveness. This is the power of forgiving another.

CHAPTER FOURTEEN:

27 Days, 7 Hrs, 7 Mins

WE HAVE ALL agreed, every one of us, to allow others the ability to have impact on us. The more we love, the more vulnerable we agree to be, the more impact we allow others to have in our lives. I agreed, from the moment I read Adam's first email, to be open, vulnerable, caring, tender, honest, and respectful. Yet, in the last week of our relationship, as Adam worked his way through his thoughts and feelings, I did not fully share the depth of my mounting anger and frustration with him. I wanted to give him time to work through what he wanted to do. When he came out of his man-cave and gave me the news of his intentions, I wrote him back:

SUBJECT: ***Sitting in the Fire***

> *I love you. When I am not lost in self-pity, and maneuvering inside of myself with agendas, that is the final truth. It doesn't matter if you are lost in fear and shut down by your negative ego. It doesn't matter if you throw us away…I will love you, I just won't be with you.*

You might not like most of what I write here, but as I re-listen to my intensive with my mentor, I pick up more of what I missed the first time through. One of the things I don't always do is speak my whole truth. I intend to do that here, as we sit in the fire together.

One of your requirements for sitting in the fire, is that we touch. Interestingly, in the first hour of our intensive time together, my mentor and I spoke of touch. He told me that the reason I love to touch, the reason you love to touch, is that it takes down the masks we wear. When we touch each other there can be no masks. So sit with me on the couch, knees touching, holding hands, and listen to my truth.

As I moved myself out of self-pity and hurt I began to think about you. I am so sorry, my love, that it has taken me so long to think about the pain you must be in. The pain must be considerable, maybe even horrible, for that is the type of pain you would have to be in to throw away our gift from the Goddess, "us."

Knowing, from my viewpoint, that you are in the quagmire of negative ego and your "lesser self," I went to find you. I went into meditation to find you in the "more real." You were/are sitting alone on a rock that seems to have roots (I don't understand what I am seeing but perhaps you do. Perhaps you recognize this place where I found you). You are looking out over forever. You look up at me with the saddest eyes. You say, "I'm lost."

I sit down next to you and together we are looking out over forever. I will sit with you for as long as it takes for you to know you are not alone. You don't want to trust that you are not alone. You push me away deliberately, I know it. You want me to be strong enough to fight the parts of you that do not trust love anymore. I will, here in the "more real." You need to fight, and then love, the parts of you that do not want to trust a woman ever again. The parts of you that rage and rage. The parts of you that are so hurt, so filled with fear that you are not sure you will really surface again in this lifetime. So I will sit with you. I know about these parts of you. I have read them in-between the lines of your missives. I have seen them in your self-doubt.

Everyone needs someone to believe in them, no matter what. I believe in you, even if we are apart. I will love you even when you tell me not to.

Our instant connection, how we hold hands is such an intimate fit, the joy we have in each other's presence, the dreams we began to dream, the challenges we faced together...how could I not love you? I believe in you and I believe in us. You say there is no "us" in your heart. That, my love, is your choice. Yes, it is a choice...because you see everything fit into place. The great wheel of life turned and the Goddess gave us to each other. You say, "No thanks."

I say that it is hard to make clear choices on the wrong side of shame, on the wrong side of deservability, and in the stranglehold of your fear of not being enough for me. As you said, it is easier just to end "us"...so you did.

I can't change that decision, only you can. For my part, I wish you had waited to consider ending "us" until after you completed your internal work. I wish you had walked though the healing gates and ended your shame. I wish you had waited until you stood on the other side of your fears and doubts to know you deserve. I wish you had waited until you knew, really knew, how much you are. For reasons I may never totally understand, you didn't. Fear closed your heart down to me, to you, to us.

• • •

Love, we are never really ready for the type of love we could have had, but we can be ready enough. But both parties must jump off the cliff together. Holding hands and screaming with excitement and fear, all the way into the next paradigm of love.

This is what my mentor said about us. "I am faced with me, yearning for connection. I am faced with you, yearning for connection. We desire to create a reality that is not of separation. What we feel/want is honest-to-god respect. What we have/want is love. These things are a celebration of who you are...a celebration of who we are."

He went on to say: "A part of us (both of us) says no to our love. 'I can't, it is not safe,' said our negative egos and lesser selves. The presence of the other is a reminder that the other has the same thing going on at some level. The question is, 'What kind of impact do I want to have on your adventure of life?' The greatest impact is to challenge myself to be vulnerable. The greatest impact is to challenge myself to say and experience what is true in the moment."

In this moment, it is to express all of me to you. I need to express my need of connection without expecting you to be my connection. To be vulnerable in myself, to let my vulnerability be expressed even if I do it without touching you. In this resonance of connecting, it changes everything. I can sit with you in meditation, in the "more real." I can hold your hand and hold the space for "us." I can feel your head on my breast and the tears on your cheeks and love you.

• • •

As I sit in the fire on the couch with you, I need to let you know how angry I am with you. You gave us up without a fight. You just threw us away. You let your fear of not being enough for me warp and twist your thoughts. In a matter of days you collapsed into your own personal house of horrors, and decided we were not worth the risk. I can track it in your missives to me. One moment you are telling me, "I love receiving your missives…they let me know you are not that far away and I can connect with you…I was writing to a girlfriend about us and was telling her that I am going to work on that negative ego and open my heart…get back into my heart." Then, one missive after another, you pulled away and became less than your true self. I hope this makes you mad, really mad, not at me, but at the parts of you that are so willing to throw the goodness of life away.

Still on the couch with you, I truly wish I was sitting on your bed in Kathmandu and looking in your eyes, the traffic roaring outside, touching you and reminding you that love is available to you—all you have to do is say yes. You don't trust your heart, you have stopped listening to it. You don't trust what we have, and could have. I feel you shrinking and settling again. It won't work, Adam. Hurt can come no matter how much we shrink, but it is worse because we know that in running from the possibilities of hurt, we failed ourselves. You can get lost in another relationship. You can try and love another woman. But until you face these things in yourself, you will be lost.

Stop it Adam. Just stop it. Say no to the parts of you that are so frightened. Love them. Hold them. Forgive them. Do your work, but not in your own head. Get help. No one who really grows does it alone. Work with whoever is wise and whole. Don't lean on friends who expect less than magnificence for you. Lean on friends who want you to have a whole and fantastic life.

You tell me that your life will not be with me. I can do nothing but accept that. As I said my love, "both" must jump off the cliff. But I can fight for you, if not for us…and I will. I will go into the "more real" and offer you what I can. You are lost. I recognize the symptoms, because I have no idea how to be in this new paradigm. Living in the new paradigm means being lost and learning more each and every day. Some days I am literally immobile, not knowing who I am in this new place. I was hoping we could be lost together, it's more fun that way. But you say no.

Do you know Adam, there is no place in the world I wouldn't have gone to be with you? Do you know that there is nothing you lack? Do you know that everything I ever wanted in a man is in you? I know now I must give to myself what I wanted from you, and that fits for me. What really burns me is that you won't let me love you. In the vernacular, that is just F&^ed.*

So Adam, decide who you want to be and what voices in yourself you are going to listen to. Decide. My dearest love, the answer is always more love and more healing. Your negative ego, from my perspective, is winning.

What would your eyes say if they could speak…?

Life is a gift.

Love is a gift.

We are a miracle…one that you gave back.

Love doesn't wait for us to be ready.

For the type of love we have, we are never ready but we can be ready enough.

Clearly I wasn't ready. Clearly you were not ready. How sad for both of us.

Being loved has been our dream, but our legacy lies in being loving.

So Adam, you asked, "Will you sit in the fire with me?" The answer is yes. Will I continue to love you? Yes. Will I move on now and open myself to someone whom I can love? The answer is yes.

I am out of words. You ask is it okay to still connect with me and be a "travel buddy"? The answer is no. I don't want to be your buddy. If the day ever comes where you want to once again risk love with me—please—with all my heart, I say please, write me a love missive and let me know.

K

Step Toward Independence

Just as I asked Adam to do, I looked at all of the aspects of me that were in pain and I let them feel their pain and vent their rage. Sometimes I did this on paper, which I later destroyed, and sometimes in meditation. The key was to allow them voice, and then healing. When I'd done these things and forgiven myself, I was ready to forgive Adam. Until I learned about forgiveness, I had never realized how holding on to my anger toward those who had hurt me kept me from happiness. By not forgiving Adam, I would have inflicted pain upon myself, more than he ever could.

When we refuse to forgive someone, it is ourselves we hold hostage, not the person we refuse to forgive. Locking ourselves within walls of anger, victimhood, martyrdom and fear, we stubbornly stand guard. The price of freedom is forgiveness. This was neither a quick nor an easy lesson for me in the beginning of my journey of growth. Now, many years later, it has become easier. In the beginning, I discovered I could forgive in phases. In the first phase, I had to discover and forgive the "why"—*the* reasons behind someone's behavior. In the second phase I could, when I was ready, forgive the behavior itself, the "what."

It is important to understand, that in order to change you do not have to forgive "what" they did. Perhaps what they did is unforgivable to you. You can, however, forgive the "why." That can set you free. Do not get stuck on "what" they did and remain their prisoner forever. Set yourself free, by forgiving "why" they did whatever it was that they did.

I knew in order to forgive Adam, I had to remember what I knew about his unresolved past. Knowing his history helped me understand the abused child within him, that didn't feel he was "good enough" to be loved. I have great compassion for the child he once was, the child that was judged never to be "good enough." This knowledge, understanding, and compassion prepared me to forgive the "why."

Understanding myself and having compassion for myself, helped me have compassion for Adam. Having forgiven myself made it so much easier to forgive him. I could forgive "why" Adam said no to our love. Why he turned away from the very thing he longed for: love, intimacy, and a woman who would not betray or abandon him.

Forgiving the "why" does not excuse behavior, nor does it justify the pain and scarring caused by another. But it is a way to begin to forgive and let go. Adam was never abusive in our relationship. However, you might be in a relationship with someone that is. Perhaps the woman in your life belittles you, and strips you of your sense of self. Perhaps the man in your life is emotionally unavailable, thus abandoning you. No matter what the behavior, look to the "why" and forgive that.

> **Secret:** ***When we forgive the "why," we can open the door to forgive the "what." You may never be able or willing to forgive the "what." That is okay. What was done may have damaged, scarred and hurt you. Not forgiving the "why" continues the hurt. If you are ready to forgive the "what" then do that as well.***

If I could, I would create an icon and insert it here, and have it flash a red light endlessly. Everywhere you go it would flash red until you graced your life with letting go and forgiving.

This next *Homegrowth* is the ultimate secret to having the love you always wanted.

> **Secret:** ***Forgiveness is the ultimate secret in creating the love you always wanted.***

Homegrowth 7: Forgiving Others

1. Bring to mind someone you have not yet forgiven. When you are ready, use the *Forgiveness Meditation*, page 219, from the *Meditations* section. Adapt the meditation by replacing "the unforgiven you" with the person you have now come to forgive.
2. You might do the meditation several times to forgive the "whys" of the behavior that hurt you. You will know how many times you need to do the meditation by monitoring your feelings.
3. In your own time, use the adapted meditation again to forgive the "what"—the actual behavior that hurt you.

Forgiving Adam set me free!

I was now ready to change the belief, *No man will love me the way I want to be loved.* The subtext, the reason for that, is that I am "too much, too intense" and the opposite end of the spectrum, "my love is not enough."

After completing three of the four steps in the Change Process I know myself, my motivations and my strengths and weakness around this belief. I have forgiven myself for the harm that holding the belief did to me and to Adam. I had forgiven Adam. Doing so helped me create a new kind of love life, one that was more than I had once thought possible. Now it was time to complete the process, allowing the freedom of a new life and the possibility, should I want it, of a new kind of love relationship.

THE LAST CHAPTER:

Change
30 Days, 2 Hrs, 6 Mins

ADAM WROTE, seeking answers to questions that haunted him. I did my best to give him those answers. It would be the last time I gifted him with total vulnerability. It would be the last time I shared the sacred within me. It would be the last time I would allow the wise woman in me to come forth to be of service to him.

SUBJECT: ***Let's Sit on the Rock and Talk***

Hello Dear Adam,

There is a full moon tonight and a lunar eclipse. It is a very powerful night and it is 2 a.m., and I am wide-awake. I was told that it is a time to use the fire of this eclipse to burn away something you want to let go of. And/or the energy can be used to set fire to a new adventure…I have done both and am at peace.

It is from this place of centeredness and without pain that I answer your questions.

You are wonderful and your life will reflect that wonder. Your integrity is gold. Your mind is probing and curious and that is a gift. Your love, oh your love Adam, is a gift beyond measure. Should love be questioned?...yes...and explored.

Do I want a man who doesn't want me for any reason? No, I value myself far too highly for that. And you, my dearest Adam, you should not feel you need to defend your decision to anyone but your own heart. My missive to you was to tell you my truth's not necessarily yours.

So, here Adam, are my answers to your questions. I have placed my answers within the body of your last missive to me.

Dearest Kimberley,

Thank you for your missive...there is a lot in it, and I have read it now many times.

My question to you, and I ask it in gratitude, is...how did you know you loved me? You say that you "knew" and it was in your heart...why then, do you distrust my heart's answer to me about our relationship so much, but trust your own? You talk as if I'm governed by my negative ego, mired in fear and doubt...and I'm not listening to my heart's desire and I've thrown "us" away...suggesting that I'm not anchored in my true self.

K: I think that from your point of view it "feels" like being anchored in your heart...but I see it differently. There is an expression...you cannot see the hologram in which you exist until you step out of it.

But Adam, it doesn't really matter what I think and feel. Your exploration must be your own. As I have said, on the other side of Shame and Not Being Good Enough, etc., (the hologram in which you exist) you will be a different human being. There is no guarantee on that side of growth and healing that you would want to be with me. There is never a guarantee, but it was a risk I was willing to take.

A: *I will do as you ask…please know that I will search my Self again, my heart, my intuition and call on my higher self for guidance about us. I will again sweep aside the fears of not being good enough, that I don't deserve true love, that I'm fearful about the age difference, not being able to have enough money to live, my other issues…and search for my truth…I will again consider my truth, my authentic self and ask my heart for how I felt and feel about you and about us. Did I feel true love? Or was it a fantasy…was it just lust and fun?*

K: All of life is based on our imagination, in the consensus vocabulary…fantasy. Fantasy/Imagination is the beginning. Fantasy then needs to be lifted to fantasia by adding joy to what was once fantasy. You ask, "How do I know it wasn't a fantasy?" But Adam, it was a fantasy, one we mutually created, one filled with love, joy, laughter, adventure, exploration, trepidation, fear, hope, desire, integrity, communications, etc. It was a fantasy and that's how all things begin in our imagination. Imagination is the most powerful tool of all the things we use to create our lives. People who have limited imagination, people who have dried-up fantasies, cannot lift life to fantasia…to joy. Those who refuse to fantasize live a day-to-day life of robots. Did you feel love towards me? Yes. It was in your touch, your smile, your eyes; it was in our essence. People who saw us together have asked about the energy and love between us. It was real and perhaps it was a magical moment in time…one to be savored and then released. I am not going to try to talk you into "us," Adam. My last missive was necessary for me to be able to walk away. I had to share everything with you. My covenant with you, the last one standing, was that I would give you all the facts and let you make up your own mind.

I told you what I believe to be true in my last missive. There is no need to belabor those truths here. If it helps at all, no one I know disagrees with my assessment and again, that doesn't matter. All that matters is what you feel, what you think and what you want. Those who know me are awed that I jumped into loving you. I don't regret it. You are a gift…thank you. But you don't want me. I get it. It took a while, but I get it.

A: *And I ask the same for you…reconsider your heart's feelings…do you think that the possibility of "us" is your fantasy? What is your agenda? You speak the words of love and loving me…but what do you feel about the money issues, the age difference, my pain…at my head telling me you're everything I asked for from the Goddess and yet, feeling that I don't love you in my heart? Why do I feel that? What does your negative ego want? Are you in your authentic self? How likely are you to change your feelings? Now and into the future?*

I have spent days doing very little else but feel and think about this. Questioning myself, questioning my agenda, questioning my lack…working with the adolescent and my child. Asking for help and healing. Demanding of myself that I stay in the new paradigm. Demanding that I stay true to loving you, if that is what I feel.

K: To honor you I will answer your questions one at a time.

Money issue: you are a talented and very smart man who has a passion to work with kids. Go do that! Be the man those children need. Will you get rich doing so? Yes, rich in all the ways that matter. Could you create an income that allowed you to participate in our relationship the way you would want? Of course. You could have a significant impact on children/adolescents, not only in working directly with them, but also with coming up with strategic ways to help many people work with them. You could, if you wished, marshal the combined efforts of many single practitioners and non-profits to change how we work with, and for, kids.

You could join forces with others in the world that had other careers before they went to work for, and with, kids. There is so much you can do and I hope you will do it. Where in the "fantasy" that I hold for you is poverty, not enoughness, emasculating you by being your caretaker? I have looked at my fear of this and then looked at you: it boils down to trusting you to take care of your own physical needs and pursuing your dreams. It boils down to me trusting that I will not "mother" another man and, consequently, will not create a man who would want that.

Age difference: If you were the one older than me this would not even be a question. Your age bias is inbred chauvinism, plain and simple. I understand it, but it is in your head and not real in my world.

Feeling you don't love me: there is nothing I can do about this. I surrender to you in this, Adam. If I don't fit for you, then I don't.

Why do you feel like you don't love me? Again Adam, I can only share my perspective. In short, it is too frightening right now to love the way we would require ourselves to love. It would mean risking everything...much more than you risked in your marriage and much more then I have risked in other relationships. It would require a level of vulnerability, humility and intimacy that is unprecedented in either of our lives. It would require a conscious decision to create a new map of loving. You told me that you came to learn about love at all levels and when you created me in your life you "called your bluff."

We co-created each other and, as I said in my missive, we have failed each other and ourselves in this. If you ask who would "require" us to do any of the things I listed above…well Adam, you and I. We would never be satisfied with anything other than the depth and breadth of love. We would never be satisfied with anything but a love that grows and deepens. You can have the love you want Adam, when you are ready—only you know when that will be. Will there be other opportunities to love the way we could have?…yes, of course. The Goddess always says "Yes." If you want to risk this again, at a time that is more right for you, you will create another woman who offers you all that you want.

Living in another country: We never decided where we would live. For me the U.S. was one of the places, but only one. I told you I would have gone anywhere we needed to go, for us both to be happy. When I said to you the whole world is an option, I meant it.

How likely are you to change your feelings? Now and into the future: My darling love, this is probably the only question you have asked that is from your heart and not your head or ego. This question is the reflection of the real fear you feel. I would love to say: Adam, I would have loved you forever. I know you need to hear and believe that. NO ONE can promise forever. I can only tell you how I feel in the moment, in every moment. I can offer no guarantees that I will love you tomorrow or the day after tomorrow. You and I spoke about this. We want guarantees. I want a guarantee. If I am going to strip myself naked in front of you, then damn it, you have to love me forever. You see how "off" that sounds? But it is what goes on in most of our hearts.

It is old paradigm stuff.

What I think you are really asking is, "Kimberley, will I be enough for you? Why should I risk this love? I need to know, really know you will love me tomorrow, because I cannot go through the loss of a love as incredible as we would create. I am afraid you will change your heart and mind when you really get to know me. Kimberley, you don't really know me and when you do, you won't love me. Then it will be too late and I will be destroyed?"

All of these thoughts come from the part of you that is hurting and needs more of your own love. A relationship is a choice every day. A new choice, every day. We don't talk about this in our societies, because we want the illusion of permanence. We don't want to have to choose anew every day. We want to be able to switch onto automatic. We want to assume that our love will thrive and the other person will be there forever. It doesn't work that way. It never has. Those people who continue to love each other, do so because they chose to do the work to understand love. They chose to do the work to understand how to uniquely love the person they are with. They choose each day to love and be loved.

As an aside, one of the moments I began to love you is when you said, "I really want to learn how to love a woman." You were speaking about how to love a woman in bed, but I heard more. You really want to learn how to totally love a woman. I believe you do. The Secret: love yourself first.

A: I have asked every couple I've met: "how did you know that he/she was the right person?" And without a change, the answer has always been: "You just know." It's in their hearts…just like you say it is in yours.

I have been in emotional turmoil ever since I wrote to you to tell you that I felt…I would be perpetrating a fraud on both of us…for me to commit my love and heart to you and to us …

K: I never once questioned your integrity in your words or in your actions. I know you wrote those words from your truth in that moment and, clearly, in all the moments that followed. You have closed down our possibilities and it is your right to do so.

A: As you know, integrity is a key value for me and, knowing that you would be falling deeper in love with me, organizing and administering my impending arrival to the USA to organize a job etc.; all of this when I didn't feel the sort of love that I believed I would feel for you…I would feel I misled you. I was a fraud and would go against my authentic self…for me, telling you of my true feelings (as I saw them) became a question of integrity as well as being true to my feelings.

I thought the presentation of the perfect woman in my life would mean that my heart would just "follow" my head…that it would be obvious that here she was…a Goddess on earth! Everything you want! Spiritual, loving, graceful, integrity, and has honor for herself and me. You have all of those things!

K: Dearest Adam, I love you. And that does not require that you love me back.

A: But my heart didn't follow my head …

Are you suggesting that the reason I don't "know" I love you is because my fears, negative ego, agendas, etc., have masked my heart's true feelings?

K: Yes, and that is the reason you don't want to love me. But again I am not going to try and convince you of anything. You can only operate on what you know now. Yes, you…we are moving on…but you can have the love you want if you do the work to heal and keep on your path. I believe in you. Adam, even when I am not with you, I believe in you. I want you to be happy even if that is without me. I want you to be free and here is the paradox: even if you chose to love me I would want you to be free. I am not talking about an open relationship; no, I want real freedom for us both. We would have had to figure out what that means because it is the new paradigm and I am lost in the new paradigm finding my way.

A: *Then, how do other people "know"? Are they better and more effective than me in uncovering their heart's desires?*

K: Adam most people don't find true love. They stop early in life looking for their true desires. They never create their heart's desire. Think about it. Look around you. Love, marriage, families, are torn apart all the time because negative egos, fears, agendas get in the way. All of humankind wants to love and be loving. So why do so few of us create it? For others, why do we create it only to lose it? Why are so many of us convinced that "it only happens in the movies"?

If that is true, that we all want love, why are most people settling for what they have, rather than for what they fantasized, imagined, dreamt? Why are so many millions of people without the love they seek? Why are so many lost and alone? Adam, think.

The people you speak with who love each other are the rarefied, relatively speaking, few. Are most people better at "knowing" than you? No Adam, most are caught in the same paradox: they cannot see or act beyond their fears, shame-based life, etc. Most of all because the vast majority of us do not love ourselves, by extension we cannot love another as we might wish.

NO Adam you are not lacking in this, you are one of the rare ones who will look beyond your pain and your ego to find the answers. You will find the answers inside of yourself Adam. It begins with self-love. Risking redundancy if you will do the work, End your Shame, Heal your belief that you do not deserve and Stop feeling not good enough; you will find the man you always wanted to be…one who touches his greatness. The answers you seek Adam are in these healings. If I leave you with nothing else, then let my gift to you be my love and these doorways to your self-love.

A: *Is the reason you "know" because you have transcended those fears and the negative ego?*

K: The reason I know is because I have had help, lots of it. Yes, for the most part I have healed those issues. When my fears rear their ugly heads again, I know what to do. Still Adam, even though I KNOW what to do, I get help. I don't have to do it alone. It is more elegant to move through my fears when there is someone else throwing their energy in with mine. It is more elegant when someone, not stuck in my hologram, can help me see myself. And Adam, I simply chose to love you. I wanted to love you. It feels right to love you. What I have learned is that it doesn't require a single thing from you other than for you to be yourself…it is my gift to you.

A: *Or is it just because your heart tells you? Did I misinterpret my heart? Agreed, we didn't spend too much time together and one woman I met said that she…"knew that this was the man she would spend the rest of her life with" after one week …*

K: Adam, time is an illusion, a game we play to keep our minds going in one direction or another…past…future. Love happens when we allow it, when we are willing to receive it. Not a second before.

A: *So you can see, that if you are imploring me to question my heart, there are many questions…and what about the exigent fact that the questions are there…does this mean that the planets are not aligned?*

K: Adam, given your unresolved past history, given your courageous journey into yourself it is only logical that you ask questions of me, of us, of yourself. Those questions are also weapons of separation from love. It makes sense that the "questions" are the weapons your negative ego would use to haunt you.

A: *Shouldn't I, and shouldn't "we," just know?*

K: Ok, let me tell you a story one of my mentors told me to illustrate the fact that "You cannot see what is not in your reality." When Magellan first anchored his ships offshore and got into the rowboats to get to shore, the Indians thought they were gods because they could literally not see the ships. So these men who walk upon the water or appear out of thin air must be gods. Ships were not in their reality. It was only after their shaman, who himself had to spend lots of time staring out to the sea from which the gods came, began to sense something different. He, with patience, began to use all his senses, which finally allowed him to perceive the ship. He then in turn drew pictures of the ship in the sand. Teaching his tribe to see, step by step he taught them to see what previously was outside of their ability to perceive. You can't see what is not in your reality. Think of it in simplistic terms. You learn a new vocabulary word and suddenly everywhere you look the word is being used. Was it not used before? Of course it was, it just was not in your reality and you could not perceive it.

As humans, you and I undergo an amnesiac experience...we call that birth. When we arrive, we forget all of the promises we made to ourselves and all of the lessons we have decided we would learn. Instead, we stumble through life until we are blessed with a wise one, a shaman, to step by step take us into a new world. In short, opening doorways to perceptions.

In America we say, "You can't get there from here," meaning from where you stand right now your negative ego, fears, shame-based life, keeps you from perceiving the love we might have shared. You cannot see what is not in your reality. You cannot "know" if you are not wired to know. You cannot "know" when you are standing inside your fear. Like the shaman drawing the picture of the ship, as you grow you will draw a picture of the love you want and more, you will be able to create it and manifest it.

You gave yourself a huge nudge in that direction. You said to yourself by creating me in your life, "Hey Adam, it is not over for you." You don't have to settle. There are women out there who have everything you want. You gifted yourself with me so you would have hope. You gifted yourself with me so you would do the work even when it gets hard, as it is now. You gifted yourself with me as a way of demonstrating that you do love yourself more than you thought.

When I came into your life Adam, I changed your destiny.

When you gifted yourself to me...if only for a moment in time...it reawakened the sensuous woman in me. When you gifted yourself to me, I remembered to dream of working with a man, side by side, to change our world. When you gifted yourself to me, I felt what it is like to be loved, really loved. You never have asked me Adam, why I think you loved me…if only for a moment…it was in your eyes Adam…it was in your touch…it was in your kisses. Yes, Adam you changed me with your love. Thank you for that gift. I will cherish it, always.

A: *In my book on intuition, it tells me to follow my instinct…if there are ifs and buts…then it isn't right. Should I ignore these?*

K: You cannot see what is not in your reality. When you look through the veils of fear, shame, etc., nothing can be seen clearly. Stop looking Adam. I set you free. Turn inward, not to think about me or us, but rather to heal yourself, for yourself.

A: *As you can see there are many questions, that I don't have answers for…there is much work I need to do. I understand you don't want to be my Buddy…and that you are seeking love only.*

My question? Will I, from my authentic self, be able to give you this gift?

K: I think it is clear you have chosen not to. From where you stand in your life, on the wrong side of fear, shame, etc., you are not going to give me that precious gift.

A: *Your questions are: What do you deserve? And if you have a guy who is not sure of his feelings for you…is that really what you want?*

K: Adam, we both deserve all of the love and all of the goodness, truth and beauty the world has to offer. It is up to us to say "yes" to those gifts.

A: *In loving kindness…Adam xo*

K: "I see you Adam." I love you. You are free.

Goodbye Adam.

That was the last missive of any import that I sent to Adam. Our love affair was over. But my work was not done.

I grieved. I mourned the loss of Adam. I lamented the loss of what might have been. I knew I had to finish the last step of the change process…changing my belief. If I did not, this kind of scenario would play out in my life again and again. I needed to change. I had spoken often to Adam about his need to change, and the same was true for me. I create my own reality and I had created a man who did not want to love me the way I want to be loved.

Much had already changed in me, after all, I had done the work to be in a new paradigm. And yet, I needed to be absolutely sure that my subconscious mind had recorded the changes, by recording the new beliefs. I needed, once and for all, to change the belief that manifested itself in Adam's and my love. I needed to change the belief, *No man will love me the way I want to be loved.* The subtext, I am "too much, too intense" and the opposite end of the spectrum "my love is not enough."

Having already completed Homegrowth 2: Discovering the Belief I Want to Change in Chapter Ten, page 148, you and I know what we wanted our new belief to be. For me it is, "*I love myself exactly as I want to be loved.*" Are you surprised? Remember, I had shared repeatedly with Adam that loving someone else always starts with loving yourself. If I create a man who does not love me the way I want to be loved, then I am not loving myself and meeting my own needs. I am operating from lack. I have a belief that does not work for me. If I have a subtext that "my love is not enough," then I am failing myself. It is I, not Adam, who needs to step up and love me. If the other subtext, "too much, too intense" looms its ugly head then I need to love myself enough to truly accept my powers and my strengths—all of them. So, let's walk this last and fourth step in the Change Process.

Step 4: Change

Working with the Subconscious

Change happens in the moment. It is an instantaneous event that can occur in any of the four steps of the Change Process. You and I may never know exactly when the change occurred, however, we can know we are different. We will see it reflected back to us in our lives. Our love lives will be different, more satisfying, more giving, more loving and more fulfilling. As promised we can create the "love of our life," transforming our love lives forever.

Understanding more of how our subconscious mind works may make this last step easier. As I mentioned before, we work with our subconscious mind metaphorically and in my examples I used the example of a computer to make my points. However, you can use any powerful metaphor that your like. You are about to journey into your subconscious mind to access the beliefs stored there. In doing so you may want to travel to a grand library with huge Doric columns and marbles floors, or a hall of records in the county seat of some bucolic rural town. You may decide that it would be more alluring, more mystical, to journey to an ancient room of scrolls. In the meditation to follow, *Changing Your Beliefs*, I use a magnificent garden of beauty as a metaphor for our subconscious.

Once you learn the compulsory steps you can change what your subconscious mind looks like to any of the examples I have noted.

It does not make any difference what imagery works for you, it only matters that when working with your subconscious mind you *feel* your emotions deeply, you keep *intense focus*, and *consciously choose* the new beliefs.

Have you wondered how the belief you have been working with got there in the first place? Many of our beliefs, the ones our subconscious mind uses to help create our current reality, were created by us as children. Neither you nor I want a child making decisions for us, but that is exactly what is happening, unless our child's beliefs are removed, and new adult beliefs are put in their place.

Our subconscious mind, like a computer, has no opinion about its programming. It only follows orders. It does not judge or discern that the orders, in the form of beliefs, came from a child or adult. The subconscious does not differentiate who is banging on the keyboard.

In computers, the orders are given by a specific series of zeros and ones, i.e., binary code. The subconscious minds takes commands given with intense feelings, intense focus, and choice. For example, if my belief is "*no man will love me the way I want to be loved* then regardless of anything else I do my subconscious mind will make sure that belief is honored or played out in my life.

There is no escaping the power of our subconscious, but we are its boss. We only need to know how to "speak" its language and it will do exactly as we instruct. The meditation *Changing Your Beliefs* is laid out so that our subconscious mind understands the new order/belief. Your job is to feel intensely, stay focused, and to give it the new belief.

Together, step by step, we have been working on creating a new belief. One that works better than the one we want to change. For me I want to change, "*no man will every love me the way I want to be loved*" to "*I love myself exactly as I want to be loved.*"

Our subconscious minds have been paying attention to our progress. During the steps of the Change Process, we *felt* our emotions deeply, kept *intense focus*, and consciously *chose* what our new belief would be. We have been speaking its language. Now it is time to follow through and actually give it its new orders—give it a new belief to manifest in our lives. Our subconscious minds will make sure the new belief is every bit as apparent in our lives as the old. It never failed to make sure the old belief was honored and it will make sure the new belief is honored as well.

Changing our beliefs is a process that can work in any area of our lives. Consider the impact of what you have learned. You now have the tools to change anything about yourself—anything!

Changing Beliefs

I was ready; it was time. If you did the Homegrowths you are ready as well. If you did not, then get the help you need to do so. Getting help to change is one of the most precious and loving things you can ever do for yourself.

As instructed in Chapter Ten, page 148:

1. I discovered the belief that causes me such pain. I created the wording of the new belief using the same syntax as the old belief. In doing so, I metaphorically fit the new belief into the "slot" that would be vacant when I removed the old belief.
2. I knew "why" I had held the old belief in place.
3. I forgave myself for all the pain I had caused and suffered.

In all of these steps I felt my emotions deeply, kept intense focus, and made a choice what my new belief would be.

I was ready to take the fourth and final step—Changing My Belief. You are ready as well. Complete the meditation and change the belief that your subconscious mind uses to help you create your life.

Your new belief can give you the love life you always wanted. Following the steps of the Change Process can give you a new life and a new beginning.

You and I have traveled a very intimate path together. Humility, vulnerability, openness, tenderness, caring, knowing, and loving have been in every word, in every sentence. By doing so, not only have we begun to learn how to change our lives by changing our beliefs, we have begun to learn true intimacy.

Thank you for sharing this journey with me into a new paradigm of love and living. I wish for you, above all else, self-love. Then when you are ready, I wish for the love you have always wanted and deserved.

Last Thought

LOVE, between two healthy people, is always worth the risk. There is never a guarantee, and to deprive ourselves because it "might not work out" is to surrender to fear.

Adam and I jumped in heart first, and neither one of us regret one second of our intense connection. Speaking for myself, being with Adam unveiled both strengths and weaknesses in me. My commitment to the relationship demanded that I look again at my beliefs about love. In doing so, I now have a new life. My relationship with Adam was the reason I looked at myself more deeply than before.

It is my deepest hope that by sharing a piece of my life with you, as if you were my best friend, that you will create more love in your life. If there is more love in your life, then there is more love in the world, and we have both been of service to humankind.

I wish you love,
Kimberley

Meditations

WELCOME to the realm of meditation. Welcome to an ancient wonder: self-exploration through guided visualization. The following meditations are specifically designed to complete the Change Process outlined in this book. Read, learn and complete the meditations using your favorite "wordless" (instrumental) music to set the resonance. Consider recording the two carefully structured meditations in your own voice to guide your own meditation. Or, if you wish, you may go to the website, www.getlovebook.com, to obtain the same meditations guided by the author, Kimberley Heart.

Immediately following are the core elements of a meditation. The *Forgiveness* and *Change Your Belief* meditations follow thereafter. Each meditation is fully described, which means there are elements of overlap between the meditations.

Establish Your Safe Place

In order to begin your journey inward, it is important to feel safe and secure. A safe environment encourages your willingness to explore the intricacies of your unknown self.

Before you begin either meditation, you will want to create a safe place in your imagination. After you have relaxed your body and mind, imagine yourself out in nature; you can use an actual setting or one that exists purely in your imagination. For instance, you might find yourself in the heart of a forest, on the dunes of a sandy beach, or in a spring garden.

Exploring all your senses, notice what you want to see, touch, smell, hear, and feel while you are in your safe place. Remember to use color, texture, and sound to help you create whatever is right for you. You might imagine lilies floating serenely on a still pond. Or you might prefer waves that crash upon the rocks, reflecting riotous colors in the sunlight. You can create gusting winds that tear at your clothing, or gentle breezes that softly ruffle your hair. Creating a place of safety is a flexible and changing process. With each meditation, you can expand, delete, or begin anew. There is only one requisite for your safe place: a campfire will always be burning brightly, a beacon to guide you home.

Spend as much time as you need to create your safe place. Trust yourself to create whatever you need to feel safe, relaxed and at peace. When you are comfortable in your safe place, you may begin these meditations.

Meditation: Forgiveness

1. ESTABLISH your safe place as described above.
2. Choose a time and a place where you can feel safe, relaxed and will not be interrupted.
3. Sit in a comfortable position. Relax. Use any form of relaxation that works for you. There is no one right way, just a way that works best for you. Take as much or as little time as necessary.

For example, to help you relax, you might surround yourself in a bubble of golden light. Breathing in the relaxation allows your body to relax with each exhalation. Or you might like to focus on different body parts. Beginning at your toes and working up to your head, allow each part to let go and relax. If you prefer, use a yoga breathing technique. Perhaps you are most successful just allowing yourself to drift, as if you were daydreaming. Explore and discover a form of relaxation that works best for you.

[Begin your personal recording here.]

Once you are relaxed, begin to count yourself into an even deeper state of relaxation by counting backward from seven to one. Count slowly, and with each number ask yourself to go deeper and deeper into a state of relaxation and peace.

When you reach the number one, find yourself in your safe place. Allow your senses to awaken one at a time.

Reach out and touch safety. What does safety feel like? You hear the sounds of safety; perhaps the wind in the trees, or the waves upon the shore; perhaps you hear the singing of birds, or stillness. Whatever is true for you, sense safety. Smell safety. What does safety smell like? Taste safety, what does safety taste like? And gently open your mental eyes and see safety. What does safety look like? If you are sitting, stand. If you are lying down, stand. Walk around and familiarize yourself with your safe place.

Whatever your safe place is like, allow it to gather around you. Sit, lie, or stand in your safe place; just "be" for a short while. Allow safety to change you. Allow safety to prepare you.

It is here that you will come when you choose to communicate at a deeper level with yourself. Always begin and end in safety.

You have come to forgive yourself. The part of you that, for so long, has been held at bay, who's been held in prison, away from you. The part of you that you would not admit is wounded and hurt. The part of you that has been hurtful to you and others. It is time to rediscover, to find that part of you. You are ready now to forgive yourself.

You know why you held on to the belief for so long, you know why you held onto the actions for so long. You've worked with and reviewed all your payoff questions, and you understand the "why." It's time to find the you that clung to those "whys," that held on tenaciously, that locked themselves away, just out of your reach. It's time to forgive them.

So, here in safety, proclaim to yourself and the universe what you are about to do. Put your head back and proclaim, "I'm going to forgive myself for all the harm I have caused by hanging on to this belief! I am going to forgive myself," you say, for the second time, and you proclaim for the third time, "I am going to forgive myself!"

Move to the edge of safety. Prepare yourself to step from safety across its boundary into the unknown. Making the decision, making the clear choice to forgive yourself, lift your dominant foot and step. As you walk, you are searching for the part of you you've come to forgive. As if it calls to you, you have a sense where to travel into the unknown. Walking, you trust yourself. Perhaps you walk down a gentle slope, or into a valley, or through a forest, or along the seashore, or perhaps through meadows blooming with bright flowers. Whatever the landscape, move and search for this part of you. Feel the tug, somewhere in you, and whether it moves you up or down or right or left, follow that knowing, that tug, trust your heart. Trust your knowingness.

Moving more quickly now, you move up hills, around valleys, over old tree trunks, move, following your heart, your instincts. Know you can find this part of you that you've come to forgive. There, just around the next bend, seeming so out of place, is an old, dilapidated building, crumbling, not quite square anymore. There is a door, swollen into the door jambs—you can't even really describe the color of the building, it's so faded, paint long worn away by the elements. Sense it: you know that this place, this building, holds the you you've come to forgive.

Hurry now over to the door. Place your hand on the door handle, and turn it, hearing it squeak in protest. It has not been opened in a long time. With a tug, the swollen wood releases its hold, and you fling the door wide, determined to find the one you've come to forgive. Step across the threshold, and look down the length of the building. The building is long and narrow. There are cells on the left and the right. It has been a long time since anyone has been here. Most of the doors are missing; a few leaning against walls, one or two hanging by the hinges.

Rays of light float dimly through the barred windows. Moving more rapidly, be determined to find the one you've come to forgive. Your head swings to the left and the right as you search; cell after cell is empty, and then up ahead, you notice one of the cell doors is closed. Hurrying to it, your eyes search the cell. It takes a moment, but then you see it, there, in the corner, a body. Head bowed, arms wrapped around knees sitting in this rotten, old, dilapidated prison. This must be the you that you have come to forgive!

Enough, you think and put your hands on the bars of the door and PULL—and you almost fall over. The door wasn't locked. Swing it wide, step in and cautiously moving forward, you say, "Hello."

There is no movement at first. Becoming even more concerned, you move closer and say again, "Hello? It's me. I'm sorry it took so long—I didn't forget you."

Slowly, there is movement from the lowered head. Take in a sharp breath when you look into the eyes…the eyes! Such pain! Such sorrow! You reach out but the figure pulls back. You're a little startled and you say, "I've come for you. Come now, it's time. Let's leave this prison."

The figure is the unforgiven you. It looks up at you with eyes swamped with sorrow, and pushes itself up using the wall to get to its feet. Then you see them: wounds, gaping wounds upon its body. This you, this one you have come to forgive has hurt themselves again, and again by refusing to see through their avoidance, through their blame ...

Slowly, step backwards one step at a time, this unforgiven you follows. Keep your eyes trained on them. Only able to look at your feet, the unforgiven one follows; back out of the cell, more quickly you move down the corridor. The unforgiven you moves stiffly as if it hasn't walked in a long time, but they follow. Opening the door at the end of the long corridor, the door that you haven't yet used. Pushing hard against the old rotting door, it swings wide and you step into the sunlight. The unforgiven you steps across the threshold of their prison blinking rapidly. It hasn't been in the light in a very long time.

Keep encouraging the unforgiven you forward, until you both stand in center of a beautiful plateau; perhaps it's a meadow, glade, or arbor of trees. Whichever, it is most certainly filled with the beauty of nature. The wind gently caresses you both. The birds are singing, yet this one seems to experience none of it.

Go about your work of forgiveness. There, leaning against a tree, is a wonderful walking stick. You pick it up, examine it and weigh it in your hands, for you are about to create a circle of forgiveness upon the ground. Holding the walking stick, you press one point firmly into the ground, and begin to create your circle of forgiveness. Pressing firmly, walk a quarter way around…now halfway around, creating a circle, comfortable enough for two people to stand in. Three quarters of the way around…and you close the circle, ending where you began.

Lift your walking stick up high, honoring it and somehow you know, you should place it in the circle, so you reach over the boundary line of the circle, and place it in the circle itself. Pleased with the circle of forgiveness you have created, you look at this one that you've come to forgive, and you say, "We are going to collect seven objects; each one representing one of the "whys" we've come to forgive: our avoidance, our righteousness, our blame, the guarantee we wanted from God before we would move an inch, our self-pity, our better than, and our tenacious clinging to the past."

Together seek the symbols, seven symbols, seven objects. Perhaps a beautiful maple or oak leaf. Perhaps an acorn. Perhaps a blossom. Perhaps sweet grass. Search now and choose the seven objects.

Each object you find, you hold up for their inspection. The unforgiven you looks at it through glazed, dull, dead eyes. You show the objects of your choosing, so it will understand that you know what needs to be forgiven. You understand the "why," and go about collecting your items of forgiveness.

(Pause)

Find those seven objects. At least three by now, perhaps four.

(Pause)

Five.

(Pause)

And over there, yes over there, the sixth.

(Pause)

And finally the seventh.

Take your objects now, the symbols of the "why" that you have come to forgive, back over to your circle of forgiveness. Choose where on the circle, where on the line of the circle, the seven objects need to be placed. Trust yourself, you will know. Place the first one, and then the second…the third and the fourth…the fifth…the sixth…and the seventh.

With each of the symbols now in place, choose a place on the circle to stand. Take your stand on the line that you have drawn upon the ground. The unforgiven you that you have come to forgive shuffles over, and takes their place across from you on the circle of forgiveness. Taking a breath to steady yourself, look into the eyes of this one. Face the pain, the wounds, the hopelessness and sorrow. Do not shy away now! Not after all this work! You are responsible and can forgive yourself…it's time.

With determination, looking straight into the unforgiven one's eyes, proclaim, "I forgive you!" With that heartfelt forgiveness, the circle lights up with a golden glow, a vibrant, golden glow of forgiveness!

The entire floor of the circle is surrounded in this golden light. The objects that you have placed, representing what you have come to forgive, are alight with the forgiveness that you have bestowed! Look at them, feel the compassion and regret and say, "I forgive you!"

This one looks at you and for the first time you see life in the eyes of the unforgiven one. There is a glimmer of hope, and tears stream down the unforgiven one's face.

Perhaps yours as well.

Proclaim for the third time, "I forgive you!"

As if a silent signal has occurred, the two of you as one begin to make your way toward each other. You meet in the center of the circle.

As you get closer you see that your forgiveness has already begun to heal the unforgiven you. Their wounds are beginning to heal, and you say for the fourth time, "I forgive you!" Looking right into their eyes you say, "I forgive you!" Their face changes, the wounds heal, they stand tall and for the first time look straight back at you. Startled and pleased by the impact your forgiveness has on this one, you say for the sixth time, "I forgive you!" Their eyes, now filled with gratitude, look back at you! Step forward, close the gap and take them into your arms; hold them close and whisper for the seventh time, "I forgive you."

With that seventh declaration of forgiveness, the golden light that had gathered at your feet begins to spin upward in a spiral, beginning to create a chrysalis of forgiveness around both of you. Spinning and spinning up to your knees and to your waist. Spinning, spinning around up to your chest, over your shoulders and up over your heads. A beautiful chrysalis of forgiveness has been formed. Hold tightly to this one, the one who that has been healed by the power of your forgiveness. Tighter and tighter hold this one, and with a deep breath, breathe this one back into you.

Gently, reintegrate this part of you that had been lost, that had been unforgiven. Now healed and forgiven, it is once again a part of you. You find yourself holding yourself, your arms wrapped tightly around yourself, standing in the golden chrysalis of forgiveness. Standing in the golden light. Breathe in the light (inhale, exhale). And again! (inhale, exhale). The golden light fills every part of you, every cell, travelling through your blood (inhale, exhale), as you breathe in the golden light! It surrounds every organ, all the parts of your brain, your lungs (inhale, exhale), all your joints, your bones (inhale, exhale), the forgiveness healing, healing, healing now from the inside out! (inhale, exhale). Breathing in the last bit of golden light, golden, healing light, the chrysalis of forgiveness is now a part of you, integrated in you, into every cell, into every part of your being, the healing light of forgiveness.

Allow forgiveness to continue to do its work, to continue the healing process, integrate more and more, know that you have been forgiven by yourself!

Allow forgiveness to continue to heal your body, your spirit, your emotions, your mind…every part of you…healed, healing …forgiven.

You don't know how long you stand in forgiveness, but when you come back to yourself, turn and gently walk back to your safe place.

Stepping across the threshold into safety, find a place to sit, relax, allow all that you have done to be real.

I will count from one to five, and when I get to five, you will find yourself back in your room.

One…beginning to be aware of your surroundings.

Two…becoming more and more aware, more and more aware of your body.

Three...more and more aware, hearing the sound that are around you.

Four...(Inhale) deep breath, allowing it to be real.

And five...Eyes open! Wide awake! Wide awake...and forgiven.

Just be for a moment, allowing yourself to adjust—give yourself precious moments to adjust and to begin to imagine what life will be like...*now that you are forgiven!*

Meditation: Changing Your Beliefs

HAVING ESTABLISHED your safe place, know that you can change it any time you wish. Expand it, add new things, remove things; it is yours to change as you see fit.

Choose a time and a place where you can feel ready, relaxed, and will not be interrupted. Sit in a comfortable position. Relax. Use any form of relaxation that works for you. There is no one right way, just a way that works best for you. Take as much or as little time as necessary.

For example, to help you relax, you might use some of the techniques introduced in the *Forgiveness Meditation.* Surround yourself in a bubble of golden light. Breathing in, allows your body to relax with each exhalation. Or you might focus on different body parts. Beginning at your toes and working up to your head, allow each part to let go and relax. If you prefer, use a yoga breathing technique. Perhaps you are most successful just allowing yourself to drift, as if you were daydreaming. Explore and discover a form of relaxation that works best for you.

[Begin your personal recording here.]

Close your eyes. And begin to relax. Do whatever you need to do to reach a level of relaxation that is right for you.

Once you are relaxed, begin to count yourself into an even deeper state of relaxation by counting backward from seven to one. Count slowly, and with each number ask yourself to go deeper and deeper into a state of relaxation and peace.

When you reach the number one, find yourself in your safe place. Allow your senses to awaken one at a time.

Reach out and touch safety. What does safety feel like? Hear the sounds of safety: perhaps the wind in the trees, or the waves upon the shore. Perhaps you hear the singing of birds, or total stillness. Whatever is true for your sense of safety. Smell safety. What does safety smell like? What does safety taste like? Gently open your mental eyes and see safety. What does safety look like? If you are sitting, stand. If you are lying down, stand. Walk around and be with safety. Allow safety to change you. Allow safety to prepare you.

It is here that you will come when you choose to communicate at a deeper level with yourself. Always beginning and ending in safety.

Allow safety to become a part of you. As you walk around and touch safety, think about why you've come. You have forgiven yourself for clinging to this belief for so long. For all the actions, harmful to yourself and to others, you have forgiven yourself. Forgiven, now you have come to change a belief, to be done with it. To change a belief that has been so harmful into one that will add to your life, that will add to the love and joy and happiness and intimacy in your life.

Review in your mind the old belief, and rejoice in your heart at the new belief that will soon be operating in your life.

You know that you must find your way now into your subconscious mind, the mind where you store all beliefs, and you must give it new orders in the form of a new belief. Even now you can begin to imagine what life might be like with this new belief in place.

So you take your stand, here in safety, and proclaim to the universe, "I am changing the belief (state the old belief)." And as the echo of your belief fades, you say for the second time, "I am changing my belief!" Then you say it for the third time, "I am changing my belief!"

You have recognized what belief has plagued your life. You uncovered the "why" of your tenacious hold on the belief. You have forgiven yourself for the pain you have caused others and yourself. You have done the work. You are ready to change.

Move to the edge of safety, with your dominant foot raised above the ground, make a choice that you will leave safety and travel into the unknown terrain, to find your way to your subconscious mind. And so you…step.

Move now into the unknown, whether it is a forest or valley, prairie or shoreline. Move now, move through the terrain; you are looking for a tree, an ancient tree. You seek a magnificent tree with grand roots that skim across the ground. A tree that stands solid, secure, steadfast, and mighty. Travel now deeper into the unknown. Your footsteps speed up and much to your surprise, before you realize it you are upon it. There it is, right up ahead!

You stop, stock still in your tracks, struck with the grandeur of this most magnificent ancient tree. Trying to see the top of this ancient tree, you throw your head back and look up, and up, and up. Moving closer you feel a reverence for its beauty and magnificence. You know you could sit for days and just gaze upon it. The massive roots are strong and steadfast as they run along, and then into the ground. You could lie among those roots and they could cradle you as you napped.

Moving over the roots you feel drawn to reach out your hands and to touch this ancient one. There is something very special and sacred about this tree. As you touch this tree, your tree of life, you are filled with feelings—feel.

Filled with feelings, in your reverie you place your palms against its trunk and you feel its life. Breathe in the magnificence and the beauty of this tree. With your palm on the bark, make your way around the tree. Always touching its trunk, caressing it, you slowly walk around the tree. Climbing over its mighty roots, running your hand along its trunk, feeling the life in the tree. Then your hand falls into a crevice. Curious, you peer into the crevice, but you can't see anything. Moving your fingers around, you can feel a latch. You would have missed it if your hand hadn't been on the trunk, if you hadn't been caressing the tree. With your fingers, throw the latch. As you do, a mysterious door is revealed and cracks open a few inches. Slowly you open the door, wondering where it leads.

Look down. There is a spiral staircase! It seems to be made out of the roots of the tree itself, folded in upon themselves. There on the top step is a lantern. Pick it up. As you do it lights itself!

Courage in hand, you step and begin to traverse the spiral staircase. One hand holding the lantern above your head, so as not to blind yourself. Travel down, step after step, circling around and around. Moving into the earth, into the mystery, into the unknown, you become more and more excited! Where will this journey take you? To your subconscious mind.

Traveling down, down, down, you can smell the earth now, so fresh! There's plenty of room here. The spiral staircase sweeps wider and wider with each turn, until you take the last step.

Stepping out into a dim room, you hold the lantern high so you can see the room is lined with bookcases and scroll holders. It is a library of some sort, filled with hundreds, no thousands, of books. You want to explore, but you know in your heart this is not what you are seeking.

The doors leading out of this room of stored knowledge are arched doorways. One is open. Still holding your lantern for light, you move to the light glowing from the open doorway, following the light.

Your feet move swiftly, your curiosity in full bloom. As you walk through this first doorway, almost at a trot, it occurs to you that you are in one of your subconscious mind's many libraries where it stores all the information you've ever been exposed to.

Down one corridor, and then another follow the light, always following the light. Then you see a brilliant light shining through the door at the end of a corridor...it must be daylight!

Hurrying to the end, you hang your lantern upon a hook and step out into a beautiful sunlit courtyard. The courtyard is teeming with plants. There are young seedlings, just breaking though the surface, reaching their leaves to sunlight for the first time, and trellises so old, that it is the flowers holding them up as they wrap themselves around posts and up over the roof. Huge flowering plants spread riotous color everywhere. Open-air corridors surround this courtyard on all four sides.

Wishing you had more time to explore, you move through the courtyard. You are on a mission, a mission to change your belief. Moving down one of the open air corridors, you step out into rolling hills, flowerbeds freshly turned, thousands of plants, some in pots, some in the ground. You have made it to your subconscious mind's working garden, your garden of beliefs. Plants of every size and description are everywhere! There are greenhouses with gleaming panes of glass, some with windows wide open. Some with courage plants, peeking through the open windows and reaching for the sun. There is life everywhere!

Take a moment to catch your breath, to adjust, to allow yourself to see what is in your garden of beliefs. Standing still, surveying your garden of beliefs, you catch glimpses of people, moving here and there, intent upon their work.

You move deeper into your garden and it occurs to you that you might be in the heart of your subconscious mind. Here all of your beliefs are thriving. Here is where your beliefs are honored, tended, cared for and made real in your life.

The power of your subconscious mind is such that whatever seeds you have planted here with total focus, with intense feelings and with choice, are the seedlings that have grown into beliefs. Beliefs that will be manifested in your life. Those who tend this garden have no judgment as to the beauty of a belief, or to the destructive power of a belief. They don't judge the beauty of a flower or weed any differently. They are all tended, they are all nurtured, they are all a part of you.

Explore now. Perhaps open the double doors of one of the greenhouses and walk through it, seeing how carefully each belief, each flower, is tended. Whatever environment is needed to maintain the belief, to make sure that it is evident and living in your life, that environment is provided here. There is neither discernment nor judgment as to whether the belief hurts you or helps you.

When you have explored, move back out into the heart of your garden of beliefs. There you notice, for the first time, is a worktable. The worktable might be long, made of thick planks of redwood, or perhaps it is a square table made of stone with ivy growing up its legs. Whatever your worktable looks like, move to stand before it.

Upon your worktable is a pair of gardener's gloves, a trowel or hand spade, a silver watering can, and a copper pot or bowl. Next to the copper bowl is a butane lighter that you simply pick up and click, and flame appears at the end of it. There is a mound of fresh earth, that has been worked through with all of the nutrients needed to grow a new belief. There is a small pile of little stones. There is an indelible ink marker used by gardeners to record what has been planted, on the face of each clay pot. Notice that not far from your worktable is a compost pile, known to gardeners as "black gold," for it is here that the old and dead can be transformed.

In the center of your worktable is a large plant. The plant has been moved from your garden of life into this pot. Because you worked with your payoff questions, your subconscious mind knew you were coming and brought this belief to your workspace. The plant of this belief is strong and healthy. Even though it has caused you so much pain, it continues to thrive, and will do so until you destroy it in at least three ways.

Notice that across the face of the pot, your belief is written in your own handwriting. You are the one who created the belief, and you are the one who has come to destroy it and plant a new belief. It was with total focus on your part, it was with commitment on your part, it was because you imbued emotions into this belief that the seed grew into this thriving plant. It has flourished in your garden of life. You have journeyed this far, it is your choice now: destroy this old belief!

With determination, put on the garden gloves and grab the plant by its stem right at the level of the dirt. Sense the life in this destructive belief, pull it out of the pot, roots and all, and slam it down onto your worktable!

The dirt that has clung to the roots begins to fall away, and you began to tear the plant apart! With each pull, with each tearing apart of the plant and its roots you say out loud with total focus, with total commitment with immense feelings, "I am ending this belief!" Feel the depth of pain, frustration and sorrow that this belief has caused and use those feelings to rip this belief apart. Pulling, tearing…"I am ending this belief!" Ripping off the stems from the core shaft of this plant of belief, demand, declare, "I am ending this belief!" Tearing the roots from the stalk, "I am ending this belief! I am ending this belief! I am ending this belief!" Tearing the roots and stalks, stems and leaves into bits you proclaim, "I am ending this belief!" Committed! Focused!

Catch your breath. Look at the bits of shredded belief strewn on your worktable. Take what is left of the stalks, of any flowers, of any roots, and put it into the copper pot or bowl. Holding your focus, pick up the lighter and light the flame. Move the flame over to the copper pot and ignite the bits and pieces of what was once a thriving belief. The flame catches immediately and begins to consume this old belief. Use the end of the lighter to move the old bits of plant around, so the flame catches and consumes.

Watch the flame consume and purify. Watch the changing colors, the hues of yellow and red, as the belief is consumed. Watch as the flame changes to green and blue. The flame consumes it all! Watch the twirls of smoke drifting out of the copper pot. Keeping focus, feeling your feelings, watch the last of the flames turn the belief to ash. Watch the smoke drift away.

Picking up the copper pot by its handle, and the trowel, move with determined steps to the compost pile. Stand before the compost pile, and use the hand trowel to break the ash that is within the copper pot into dust.

Dig a hole, making room in this nurturing soil for what once was a destructive belief, and is now dust. Bury the dust, give it back to the earth.

Having destroyed this belief, in at least three ways, you feel a sense of relief, but more...a sense of hope!

This old belief that has affected your life, your love, your ability to be loving, to be loved in return, to trust, or how you held men or women is destroyed. It is time to create a new belief!

So with bold strides, move back to your worktable, and notice that your subconscious mind has left you a new clay pot and a single seed. A seed waiting for you to imbue life into it! From this single seed, a new belief can grow. A belief that can change your life forever, that can permanently transform your love life!

Remove your gloves and pick up the indelible pen. Lean the pot on its side and write across the face of the pot your new belief. You are recording the new belief that will be planted in this pot. Write with bold, determined strokes, write with focus, with choice, with all the emotions you will feel when you live the life of this new belief. Do it now!

Put down the indelible pen and set the clay pot upright. Take a handful of small stones and place them in the pot so they cover the entire bottom. Take handfuls of the fresh, nurturing, life-giving earth and put it in the pot. Fill the pot halfway full.

When you are pleased with the results, turn your focus to the single seed sitting on your worktable, in the heart of your garden of beliefs. This seed has not been germinated or imbued with life. That is up to you.

Pick up the seed and place it in the palm of your hand. Knowing what it takes to create a belief, total focus, intense feelings and choice, you are prepared.

Begin to breathe life into the seed! Focus! Feel! Think about the belief you are creating. Choose! Cup your hands together and imagine your life, as it will be with this new belief! Speak the new belief out loud. Feel and push those feelings into the seed! Imagine what life will be like with this new belief. Push those imaginings into this seed. Feel the determination that you will have this new life! Speak your new belief out loud for the second time, pushing your resolve into the seed.

Claiming and demanding, state your new belief a third time, pushing the energy, the feelings, and the commitment into the seed.

With clear choice, you imbue this seed with your new belief. With focus, intense feeling and choice you breathe life into your new belief.

Open your hands and the small seed of belief is glowing with life.

Place the seed of your new belief upon the earth in the prepared clay pot. Take a moment to feel what you are doing. A new belief has been created. With your bare hands you take a handful of soil and gently place it over your seed, filling the remainder of the pot with life-giving soil. From the silver watering can, you gently water your seed of belief.

A new belief has been created.

Your subconscious mind will tend it, and provide the perfect atmosphere so this belief can grow. Pleased and excited, you look up from your work.

There in front of you, on the other side of your worktable, you see the personification of your subconscious mind. Male or female, old or young, they have watched closely what you have done and understand your orders. They nod at you. You smile and nod back.

Walk around your worktable and stand in front of them and say, "Thank you. You have been a faithful friend. You have served me without ever asking why, simply following my orders in the form of beliefs, making sure that those beliefs were honored and alive in my life. I have not always planted seeds of beliefs with conscious thought, but I am doing that now."

Your subconscious mind cocks its head to the side and nods. It understands its orders, and moves to pick up your new belief, and heads to the greenhouse, where it will nurture it and care for it, and see that it blooms tall and strong.

You will come back here to your garden of beliefs two more times. It will be an effortless journey into the heart of your subconscious mind, and you will see that your new belief grows and becomes a strong plant, that your subconscious mind will replant in your garden of beliefs in your garden of life.

Turning now, walk back through the open air corridor, across the courtyard, back into the room lined with books, and up the spiral staircase made from the roots of your tree of life. Step out of the tree into the night; whatever time of day you entered, it is now night. Put your palms upon your tree of life…thank it.

Journey back to your safe place and look up—the stars shine upon you this night. A new belief has been birthed, and planted, and will be nurtured and will grow. Stepping back into safety, your belief has already changed safety. It feels more solid, more filled with the joy and happiness, excitement, hope, and love of life!

Sit in your favorite place, beginning to imagine what life will be like now that you have permanently transformed your love life.

You know that you have made the commitment to visit your new belief two more times. Stand with it and continue to imbue it with your focus, your intense feeling and your choice. Your life has been changed forever!

I will count from one to five, and when I get to five, you'll find yourself back here, present, in your room.

One…Gently breathe in ...

Two…becoming aware of your surroundings.

Three…more and more aware of your body. More and more aware of your surroundings. You can begin to hear the sounds around you.

Four…(Inhale) deep breath, allowing it to be real.

And five…Eyes open! Wide awake, wide awake…and changed.

FOOTNOTES

1. The concept of 'lack' is a product of my work with my friend and mentor Baratta. www.opengateways.com

2. Based on The Change Process and taught by Concept: Synergy, Unlocking the Power of Changing Your Life @ NPN Publishing, Inc. PO Box 1789 Sonoma, CA 95476 www.lazaris.com

3. Nin, Anaïs. The Diary of Anaïs Nin, Volume I, ed. Gunther Stuhlmann. New York: Harvest/Hbj, 1966

4. Based on The Change Process and taught by Concept: Synergy, Unlocking the Power of Changing Your Life @ NPN Publishing, Inc. PO Box 1789 Sonoma, CA 95476 www.lazaris.com

5. Based on The Change Process and taught by Concept: Synergy, Unlocking the Power of Changing Your Life @ NPN Publishing, Inc. PO Box 1789 Sonoma, CA 95476 www.lazaris.com

You can find more information on
Kimberley's books, meditations and appearances on her website at
www.kimberleyheart.com

The meditations and other materials that
accompany this book are available at
www.getlove.com